Ma'alesh

An American Family in Cairo
1971-1975

Connie Shoemaker

Ma'alesh: An American Family in Cairo, 1971-1975
by Connie Shoemaker

Published by

Amity Bridge Books

Editing: Jen Marshall, TwinOwlsAuthors.com
Book Design: Nick Zelinger, NZGraphics.com

ISBN: 978-0-9864253-5-6 (Soft Cover)

First Edition

Printed in the United States of America

To Floyd for 68 years of cherished memories

OTHER BOOKS BY THE AUTHOR

Taste the Sweetness Later
Two Muslim Women in America

The Good Daughter
Life Stories, Secrets and Healing

Ma'alesh
Verses from Egypt

Write in the Corner Where You Are

Write in the Middle

Interactive Techniques for the ESL Classroom

Write Ideas
Inside the News
co-author Susan Polycarpou

Contents

Preface

Ma'alesh: An American Family in Cairo is a patchwork of memories from the past and observations from the present. Each piece of fabric has its own shape and character, held together by the common thread of the life-changing experience of four years in Cairo, Egypt in the 1970s.

Fifty years have passed since we returned from Cairo. How accurate are my memories of this time? Somewhat fuzzy, I must admit, but still warm, alive, and stitched together with love and the assistance of additional resources. Unfortunately, my husband, Floyd, and eldest daughter, Sonja, are no longer with me to help write this book. However, the process of composition has renewed poignant memories of both of our loved ones. Melissa (Missy), our middle daughter, offered many details of life as an eight-to twelve-year-old, and Troy, not quite three years old when we arrived in Cairo, added some priceless thoughts about his life at the villa. Friends we have retained for more than fifty years have helped to clarify our memories.

I thank my mother for saving the letters I wrote home during the first two years of our life in Cairo. She carefully placed each thin piece of airmail stationery into plastic covers and then saved them all in a notebook she presented to me when we returned to Denver. I have also saved my freelance writing about Cairo, published in several stateside newspapers and journals, and feature articles written for the *Associated Press.* Tucked away in an old file cabinet are copies of "The Ma'adi Messenger," a monthly newsletter I wrote for the American community; *Ma'alesh, Verses from Egypt,* a small poetry book printed by the American University in Cairo (AUC); and "Amel: Village Child, City Woman," the first chapter of *Seven Egyptian Women,* the project of a grant from Rocky Mountain

Women's Institute. The archives of *The Caravan* student newspaper at AUC gave me insight into Floyd's connection with his journalism students.

Many patches, many pieces, many sizes—all joined together to tell the story of our family's four years in Cairo, Egypt.

1

Welcome to Cairo

"LADIES AND GENTLEMEN, this is your captain speaking. We have now entered Egyptian airspace. Look out the windows on the left-hand side of the aircraft, and you'll see the vast expanse of the Egyptian desert stretching out before you. In just a few moments, you may catch a glimpse of one of the most iconic sights in the world, the Great Pyramids of Giza. These ancient wonders, built over forty-five hundred years ago, are a testament to Egypt's incredible history and engineering ability. Please enjoy this breathtaking view as we continue to Cairo."

Our daughters, Sonja and Missy, scurried across the aisle to peer out the window in the row where Floyd, Troy, and I were seated.

"Wow! There's nothing but yellow sand down there," Sonja said.

"Where are the palm trees?" Missy asked.

"I want camels," Troy interjected as he scrambled over Floyd's lap to press his nose against the window.

As the TWA 707 charter flight circled toward Cairo, we got a distant glimpse of three minuscule triangles obscured by gusts of blowing sand. There would be time to be awestruck by the trio of pyramids in person later in the week. Now, we returned to our seats to buckle up and prepare for the end of a twenty-hour journey—from our temporary home state, Michigan, to New York, then Italy, and finally to Cairo. It was 1971 and a long trip without available on-board entertainment, such as movies or TV. Sonja, ten, and Missy, almost nine, had read books from our carry-on bag, and Troy, almost three, had cruised the aisle, becoming acquainted with other passengers, including a few older children. Floyd had slept while I tried to corral Troy and keep him buckled in his seat.

At this point, we looked like a group of rumpled refugees wearing clothing found in a slightly upscale thrift shop. In 1971, passengers on airlines followed a dress code: professional attire, no sweats, shorts, and T-shirts allowed. My dear husband, Professor Floyd, wore a white dress shirt with a narrow blue tie, a blue-and-white striped polyester blazer with an ever-present hanky in the pocket, and navy dress pants. I sported a purple pantsuit; Missy, her favorite yellow dress; Sonja, a new red dress; and Troy, the only comfortable one, had on a jumpsuit with an easy-to-unbutton crotch for difficult trips to the airplane restroom. But he was afraid of being sucked down the toilet into space, so it wasn't his favorite place.

Twenty minutes later, the pilot cheered, "*Ahlan w'sahlan, welcome to Cairo!*"

As the plane taxied to its slot on the tarmac at Cairo International Airport, an adrenalin rush pushed aside any fatigue I felt. Before the seatbelt sign came off, I peered through the dusty glass of the window seat. Five Egyptian soldiers dressed in khaki with rifles slung over their shoulders emerged from the heat waves rising from the concrete to take positions around the portable stairs, which had been pushed up to the plane's exit door. Troy leaned over from Floyd's lap.

"Hey, Dad. Look! Guns!"

Much to our chagrin, Troy was going through a TV-inspired I-want-a-toy-gun! phase. Seeing the rifles didn't invoke fear in him, just fascination.

With a sudden burst of life and chatter, the plane came alive. We unfastened our seat belts, gathered our belongings from under the seats and overhead compartments, and squeezed into the aisle. Sonja looked up to me for reassurance, and Missy grabbed my hand, ready to explore the newness of the experience. Floyd focused on carrying Troy in one arm while clutching his briefcase in the other.

Passengers on this charter flight were American University in Cairo students, newly hired or returning faculty members, and their accompanying family members. AUC was unique in a Muslim country. It was founded in 1919 under the sponsorship of the American Mission in Egypt, a Protestant mission supported by the United Presbyterian Church of North America. At that time, it operated independently of the Egyptian government but was influenced by its mission to serve as a cultural and educational bridge between East and West.

Emerging from air conditioning to 110-degree heat stunned us as we de-boarded. I wondered if the presence of armed soldiers on the tarmac was common or if it was the result of the abrupt change in leadership of the country from President Nasser to his vice president and successor, Anwar El-Sadat. This huge political turn-around had happened just a few months before our arrival. Before we started our journey, editorials in the American press told us that when Sadat was elected, he was thought of only as an interim president, but then he demonstrated his skills in political survival. He quickly outmaneuvered rivals for power and started to dismantle the old system of government—no more wiretaps or spying on government officials. He also dismissed the followers of Nasser, who had expected to rule Egypt behind his back. He took charge of the army and released many of the dissidents who had been placed under house arrest.

Who knows what else might occur during our two-year stint here? I adjusted my focus to getting safely down the narrow stairs to the tarmac with the kids in tow. A smiling soldier, rifle still over his shoulder, helped us onto a bus that transported us to the terminal doors where we, as Americans, were welcomed like a winning Olympic team by AUC employees and the many Egyptian passengers waiting for their flights.

"Amrikani! Amrikani! Ahlan w' Sahlan!"

11

Our English-speaking assistant, Ahmed, helped us through customs, where we waited for over two hours to collect our fourteen suitcases and three lockers. During that time, the contents of each bag and locker were inspected. We had been advised not to bring any products that had a connection to Jewish companies. Since the Suez Crisis in 1956, anti-Semitic sentiment had been on the rise. In response, the Egyptian government nationalized various businesses, including those owned by Jewish Egyptians. Many American companies with Jewish ownership were indirectly affected by this action.

It was forbidden to have anything with logos or labels from three major companies. Coca-Cola was first on the list. The Egyptian branch was owned by a Jewish businessman. International Business Machines (IBM) was also listed because some of its key executives and partners were Jewish Egyptians. Third was General Motors (GM), in a joint venture with an Egyptian Jewish partner who managed Helwan Automotive Company, a manufacturer of local cars.

Evidently, we passed the test. We would retrieve, two months later, two bicycles and additional lockers with Floyd's professional books, the kids' toys, my portable Royal typewriter, and our beloved 8-track player at the seaport in Alexandria.

We boarded an airport bus destined for the Hilton Hotel. Now, it was time for our first look at Cairo, a city of four million people.

▲ ▲ ▲

September 12, 1971

Dear Mama and Daddy,

A dilapidated bus took us from the airport through Heliopolis into Cairo—past abandoned and still-used palaces, Nasser's Tomb, donkey carts, and a huge variety of dress: women with black lace veils, little boys in striped pajamas, men in long, flowing African

*kaftans, and farmers in the traditional galabiya robe... It's a
fantastic city—huge and overpopulated. The streets are full of
blossoming trees, bustling taxis, buses, cars tooting their horns,
a beautiful river with impressive nightclubs and restaurants, boats—
in contrast to the Egyptian sailboats—and streets in the main
downtown section without one piece of litter because street
sweepers clean hourly.*

*We received a warm welcome at the Hilton and were given a
three-room suite with air conditioning, which we really don't need
from six p.m. until about ten a.m. It's about ninety degrees now,
at two p.m., with cool breezes from the Nile River and beautiful,
very dry weather. Tell Grandma not to worry about heat stroke.
We'll do just fine, except in July and August.*

*Troy has been a perfect icebreaker with Hilton Hotel servants,
bazaar salesmen, and anyone else we meet. Since he's friendly to
everyone despite color, language, or dress, they all love him and go
out of their way to be nice to us.*

*At ten p.m. last night, five bouquets with each of our names
arrived at our door: peach-colored rosebuds and long-stemmed
white gardenias from the Hilton manager to welcome us to Cairo ...
Don't worry about us because we're having a great time.*

Love, Connie, Floyd, and family

▲ ▲ ▲

Excitement! Exaltation! And exhaustion! We felt welcome, special,
and winners of the AUC contest for important, newly hired faculty
and their families. The seven-hour difference between time zones
finally caught up with us. It was time for showers and inviting beds
with the sheets already turned down. There would be no bedtime
stories tonight. Floyd went to sleep within seconds, but I had to do
my usual review of events before I could sleep.

How did this all happen? Why did we decide to transplant our thriving American family from a little suburban town in Michigan to Cairo and its burgeoning population? Most importantly, we had reached Floyd's goal of a PhD. Both of us had received bachelor's degrees at Colorado State University, mine in journalism and Floyd's in education. We had married and edited the college newspaper together, and Floyd had become excited about his own career in journalism. He went on to an MA in journalism at the University of Missouri, followed by several years of teaching and administration back at CSU. Next came three years leading up to the prized PhD from Michigan State University, with an emphasis on mass communication and social change in developing countries. He was recently hired as a consultant on higher education by the Michigan State Department of Education. This job would give us some income and some time to decide what came next.

At this point, we had three children, almost three, eight, and ten, and we wanted to expose them to a world that didn't focus on two cars in the garage and competing with the neighbors in the accumulation of material things. Floyd was also determined to put his knowledge to work. His major professor, Dr. Everett Rogers, had recommended him to AUC as a candidate to establish a new master's degree program in mass communication. Floyd had informed me about this opportunity only after he had applied and the vetting process had started. My husband was sometimes short-sighted in his decision-making.

Two years ago, he told me he had applied for a one-year position at a university in Seoul, South Korea, and had been accepted. I had to remind him then that Troy was only one year old; there was no way we would move to South Korea with a baby.

After I had time to think about it, the program at AUC seemed like a perfect fit for Floyd's degree and his enthusiasm. However, I needed to know about family life in Cairo. Was it safe for children? Where would we live? Where would the girls go to school? What health concerns would we face? What opportunities for teaching and writing might I have? I wasn't just going along for the ride as a wife and mother. This could be the promise of a new chapter for me. I had supported Floyd for his degrees with teaching and journalism jobs in the university towns we lived in, but I was eager to continue my writing career and have my own unique cultural experience.

▲ ▲ ▲

It was our first dawn in Cairo. We woke up to the echoes of an electronic Muslim prayer resounding electronically from one mosque to another throughout the city.

"*Allahu akbar! Allahu akbar!*" God is the greatest! God is the Greatest.

When we arrived in Cairo the day before, we hadn't realized that it was a very important date, September 11, our sixteenth wedding anniversary. The seven-hour time difference and our travel excitement had made us forget the day we had officially begun our long-awaited marriage. I reminded Floyd of the date with a wake-up kiss and got the kids out of bed and ready for a family celebration. Sonja and Missy swam in the Hilton's outdoor pool, and we had a breakfast of French pastries, fried eggs, and our first tastes of mango juice. We felt like royalty in this posh hotel. It was a far cry from the nights we had spent at Motel 6s while traveling across the United States.

Troy happily explored the hotel lobby, restaurant, and elevator. Even though his adventures stretched my patience, the employees and guests were friendly and encouraged him to have fun. I think his antics were so well tolerated because he could be mistaken for an Egyptian, with his dark brown hair and tan skin. I was later told that little boys are highly valued in Muslim societies and are allowed to misbehave within reason because sons carry on the family name and lineage. They are the providers and protectors of the family. For the most part, women are expected to focus on domestic roles. In contrast to Troy's reception, Sonja and Missy's fair skin and blond and brunette hair drew many polite comments.

"What beautiful daughters you have!"

They were expected to behave with decorum. And they did!

We would remain in the hotel for a few days until an apartment was ready for us in the southern suburb of Ma'adi. The girls started school the next day at Cairo American College, CAC, riding with other new students on a special bus that took them from the Hilton to Ma'adi. They left the hotel with some first-day apprehension but well-armed with Hilton-packed box lunches.

When they returned from a nervous but exciting first day, the first thing Missy said was, "Yuck, Mom. Guess what was in the sandwiches? Some meat that looked like a tongue!"

Sonja responded, "It was *tongue,* Missy."

▲ ▲ ▲

The university continued to treat the new faculty as VIPs. They packed our first week with orientation meetings, teas, luncheons, and a tour that included the Egyptian Museum, the Sphinx, and the pyramids at Giza, much higher and wider than anything we could have imagined from our airplane's perspective.

We were more than ready to get settled after all this activity. It was finally time for our personal university expediter, Ahmed, to take us on a visit to Ma'adi. Because we had three children, we were promised a villa as soon as a Chinese professor and his family moved out. For now, we would live in a three-bedroom apartment in this nicely planned upscale suburb. Ahmed, who was reminiscent of a real estate agent trying to sell us on a property, extolled the beauties of the flowers, trees, grassy *midans,* central plazas for radiating roads. He also told us Ma'adi had two excellent doctors who made house calls and that CAC was just six blocks away. A small area of shops was close by on Road 9. He drove down the road to show us Gomaa

Brothers Grocery, Ayyad's Bicycle Shop, the Ma'adi "supermarket," and the Misriki Pharmacy.

"Just like America," he said.

Like many American towns, the railroad had played a role in developing Ma'adi, but its origins were unique to Cairo. In 1904, Ma'adi's development was spearheaded by Jewish families through the Egyptian Delta Land and Investment Company, which established urban planning emphasizing green spaces. Over the years, the garden suburb had attracted a diverse population, including Egyptians, Brits, French, Greeks, Italians, Jews, and now Americans. Mixed in with historic villas and commercial buildings were newer apartment houses.

"Your new home here," Ahmed pointed out as he parked in front of an attractive two-story concrete building the university had built for its American faculty and their families. Our apartment was being painted, so we couldn't go inside until the move-in day, but the outside looked welcoming. A large patio on one side of the building was a perfect place for the younger children to ride tricycles and play. We would have three small bedrooms, a living room, a kitchen, a dining area, a bathroom, and a balcony that faced the street. The apartment's rent would be deducted from our housing allowance. Along with the apartment, we would be assigned a cook-*suffragi,* or general servant. At this point, I couldn't imagine having a servant and wasn't sure I'd know what to do with him or her. The apartment house also had a *boab,* a doorkeeper, who carried packages, called taxis, and provided security, in addition to a switchboard operator and a gardener.

In the meantime, Floyd was busy getting his professional life settled. Part of the new faculty orientation included an official tour of the campus situated on Tahrir Square, a historic public location that symbolized liberation and protest. A bus picked up new faculty, all male, and their wives from the hotel. It was a school day, so older children of faculty were not included. Troy was the only child to join the group.

We quickly arrived at Tahrir Square, which appeared to be the busiest, noisiest, and most crowded site in downtown Cairo. It was near government ministry buildings, hotels, and commercial areas, the National Cultural Center, and the Egyptian Museum. Information from our new faculty packet said:

▲ ▲ ▲

"In no other place and at no other time has the collective voice of the Egyptian people ever been more amplified and passionately expressed as it has been in Tahrir. It has symbolized liberation for six consecutive generations."

▲ ▲ ▲

Circling the Square was a circus of taxis with honking horns, rickety buses, little Fiats, big Mercedes cars, braying donkeys pulling carts, bicycles, an occasional truck carrying an unhappy camel in the back, and people taking their lives at risk by scooting between the traffic. Our bus stopped at a huge ornate iron gate. It was pulled open by an Egyptian in dark pants and a white shirt. Once inside, we stepped off the bus to a haven of serenity amid the chaos of Tahrir. The campus, with a population of only one thousand students, was a walled-off, five-block garden oasis with a converted palace as its focal point. The university guide who met us said the palace housed central administrative and faculty offices. Classroom buildings and Ewart Hall, a large auditorium, were nearby. This would be Floyd's first and never-again office in a palace. Khairi Pasha Palace, constructed in the 1860s for the Egyptian Minister of Education, was the original university building. It was acquired by AUC in 1919. In contrast to the palace were outdoor basketball and tennis courts, gardens, and

a fountain area. Floyd, who had a political science department orientation earlier, took Troy's hand to explore this part of the campus
so I could join the group.

Walking around the campus was like being transported to a
street in Paris. Women students were dressed in the latest European
fashions, and the men wore Western-styled shirts and trousers. No
one wore *galabiyas,* veils, sandals, and no bare feet were seen. At
first glance, it appeared that only rich, upper-class Egyptians could
afford to attend this university. That was partially true. Our guide
told us tuition fees at the university had always been relatively high
compared to other universities in Egypt but AUC had increasingly
opened its doors to students who were not part of Egypt's traditional
elite through merit-based scholarships and financial aid initiatives.
Now, at the beginning of the 1970s, it was beginning to be a hub for
cross-cultural exchange and education in the region. International
students came from neighboring Arab countries, as well as Europe,
North America, Asia, and Africa. The university also offered
programs specifically designed for non-Egyptian students interested in
studying the Arabic language and culture.

How was it possible for this American-style university to exist in
Cairo? When Floyd and the entire family were interviewed in Michigan, the AUC representative gave us a "Welcome to New Faculty"
document that outlined the unique cultural relations agreement
established between the Egyptian and US governments. It explained
that AUC was "held in such high esteem that Nasser, at the time of
the 1967 war with Israel, signed a special protectorate for it."

Our guide took us into a classroom to introduce us to an Egyptian
professor of history. In his lecture, he revealed that the "special protection" referred to in the document was a form of sequestration.

When the university was founded in 1919, under the sponsorship
of the American Mission in Egypt, it operated independently of the
Egyptian government but was influenced by its mission to serve as a
cultural and educational bridge between East and West. The original

agreement with the Egyptian government provided a framework for its operations and its relationship with the host government.

Then came the big change. Throughout the 1960s, Nasser had played the US against Russia while promoting Arab nationalism. His ability to secure arms from Moscow while receiving economic aid from Washington exemplified this diplomatic strategy. When the US supported Israel during the 1967 Six-Day War, President Nasser ordered the university to be seized by the government and placed under control by Egyptian administrators. Several members of its faculty, particularly those who were American citizens, were dismissed or faced restrictions due to heightened anti-Western sentiment and suspicion of foreign influence.

Egypt stopped short of nationalizing the university because it was partially supported by money owed as repayment of loans made by the US Agency for International Development.

Our tour guide was quick to emphasize the new government's recognition of AUC's contributions to higher education and cultural exchange. Already in this year, 1971, there was a shift toward more open relations with the US. Sadat was seeking economic assistance from America while distancing Egypt from the Soviet influence. In the process of dismissing Russian aid and turning toward the West, AUC's role became more important. It wasn't offering dollars in aid, but it was offering education to Egyptian leaders who could assist in developing the country. Evidently, this was one reason many new American faculty had been recruited and why we were so warmly welcomed. It was AUC's goal to add bachelor's, master's, and diploma programs in engineering, management, computer science, journalism, mass communication, and sciences, as well as establishing research centers in Egypt. This initiative gave purpose to Floyd's recruitment.

▲ ▲ ▲

Two days after our Ma'adi tour with Ahmed, we moved from the Nile Hilton to our new home in the Cairo suburbs. Our suitcases and trunks had already been transferred to the apartment. Sonja, Missy, and Troy were all excited to see where we would be living. When we turned the knob on the door, we were welcomed by a beaming, rotund Egyptian man in a white cotton *galabiya* and a small knit skullcap. The well-pressed, shoulder-to-toe shirt made his dark, Nubian skin even more striking. His name was Salim, the official cook the university had assigned to us. We introduced ourselves and immediately became Madame, le Docteur, Master Troy, and Mademoiselles Sonja and Missy, honorifics expressed with a smile and a slight bow. As a son, Troy was the most important child and more valued than our daughters, so when Salim introduced me to others, I received that special title *Om* Troy, the mother of Troy.

Salim bragged about speaking half Arabic and half English; however, it was more nine-tenths Arabic and one-tenth English. He came in at seven-fifteen a.m. daily to make breakfast and the girls' lunches. His other duties included shopping, cooking all meals, bed-making, sweeping, dusting, and mopping, which he tried to shirk by just dusting the floor with a large feather contraption. Our bonus was his good cheer and his love for children. He delighted in playing hide and seek with Troy.

Salim's role included the daily tasks that all Egyptian cooks fulfilled: going to the market (accomplished on a bicycle), preparation of three meals, and house cleaning. Salim worked from before breakfast to seven or eight p.m., six days a week, taking off on Friday, the Muslim day of prayer, and Sunday, the Christian holy day. Salim earned the equivalent of seventy-five dollars a month, subtracted from our AUC allotment. The range for cooks was seventy to ninety dollars a month, depending on their skills and duties. Middle and upper-class Egyptian families paid less and required more time and added duties, so the diminishing *suffragi* class preferred to work for Americans or other foreign families.

21

Back home in the States, I didn't have the luxury of household servants. I soon learned that Salim was a necessity, not a luxury. Marketing took about two hours each day, with every item on the grocery list obtainable only in small quantities from a variety of tiny shops in the marketplace. His chores were well-worth his salary, even if he had a coffee with a fellow cook along the way. Faced with each day's shopping list, he would visit several fruit stands to compare the price of winter oranges, choose a meat shop with refrigeration, watch the butcher grind the beef, and hopefully, first inspect the grinder for cleanliness. Then he would return home loaded with groceries in string bags.

Back in the kitchen, his initial chore was soaking the Nile-washed fruits and vegetables in Rabso (the local Tide) or in permanganate and rinsing them several times, boiling the milk, which usually came from a *gamusa,* a water buffalo, picking the small pieces of twigs and rocks from the large grains of sugar or rice, and sifting the flour two or three times to refine it and to remove foreign particles. We were quite lucky in that first month not to have suffered from any severe stomach upsets, affectionately called Gyppy tummy or the Pharaoh's revenge. Vaccinations or updates had prepared us for major diseases, like cholera, tetanus, diphtheria, polio, and typhoid fever. Cholera, particularly prevalent in Cairo, required frequent updates.

As the first few weeks passed, I was frustrated with my inability to communicate with Salim. My twice-weekly Arabic classes weren't working quickly enough. I would practice my best kitchen Arabic, and he would happily correct my pronunciation. In the meantime, Salim merrily cooked up a storm of fatty meals for us. He served pancakes rolled around ground meat bubbling in thick tomato and cheese sauce; *ful* beans inside round pillows of bread, and anything he could fry in *ghee,* a clarified *gamusa* butter. It was a pity the number of water buffaloes it took to produce this oily substance. And how do you milk a water buffalo? I tried to make my desire for simple food known to Salim, to explain that I did not want to become *kbira,* big or fat.

Salim just laughed and said, "*Maʿalesh! Kbira helwa,*" never mind, fat is beautiful.

One evening, he served the same fatty entree for the third time that week. We passed the overflowing dish of tomato sauce and meat around the table quickly. Floyd, afraid of displeasing the cook, took a big helping. Sonja and Missy took a tablespoonful, and I passed the dish to Troy, who was royally seated on a large pillow atop a dining chair. Troy wasn't as shy as we were about criticizing our only source of food. He picked up the little silver bell we were supposed to ring when we needed Salim.

"Yuck! I don't want this!" he shouted while shaking the bell back and forth.

Salim came running into the dining room, looked around the table at the meager servings on our plates, and started crying.

Wiping his eyes, he said in his best English, "Salim no good. Madame no eat. Family no eat."

"*Maʿalesh,* Salim," I said. "We'll work it out."

I am learning that "*maʿalesh*" is the most versatile Arabic word in the vocabulary of the average Cairene. Among the numerous meanings, "*maʿalesh*" can signify "never mind" to wave off blunders; "it's OK, it will pass" to show care and support; "don't worry, just be happy" to encourage someone feeling depressed, or "it's alright, no harm done" to diffuse tension. "*Maʿalesh*" is more than just a word. It embodies resilience, empathy, patience, and adaptability, essential traits for navigating life in Cairo's fast-paced yet chaotic environment.

▲ ▲ ▲

As the months slipped by, Salim learned to accept the simpler food we wanted, aided by the experienced cook from a neighboring apartment, who knew more about the crazy quirks of Americans. When canned tuna appeared on the local black market, I had him buy enough to last for a year. I also discovered a good source of powdered milk, which proved a substitute for the *gamusa* milk, so the kids could have the only cereal available, cornflakes, every morning. Oh, how they missed the Fruit Loops and Frosted Flakes, which were not as healthy as plain old corn flakes but familiar food. Things began to look rosy when Salim began broiling fish or roasting or frying chicken each week.

One morning, when Salim had been with us for almost three months, he failed to appear at six-thirty a.m. One of the other university cooks came and said, "*En sha'allah,* God willing, tomorrow Salim come."

Two days later, Salim arrived, apologetic and with a handful of pill bottles. As far as I could understand, he suffered from some sort of stomach disorder. The doctor had prescribed medication and a simple diet to lose weight.

"Now Salim eat like Madame," he explained. Then he tapped his skullcap and added, "Madame, *kwayiss auwy,*" meaning that I was very wise.

Arab Tents

In wintry Michigan, I dreamed
of loving you in Arab tents
and harem rooms. I'd dress in veils
and gauzy pants with one bright gem
aglitter in my navel's eye.

In sultry Cairo, love is given
in rooms of sterile modern style.
No veils, no gems, just you and me
and sun-warm touch that stays the same
across the globe six thousand miles.

2

Settling In

THESE FIRST WEEKS, according to our university welcome manual, would be the honeymoon stage of cultural adaptation. How true this was! The newness of our surroundings, intriguing experiences, and friendly encounters were exhilarating and fascinating. We were given warm Egyptian welcomes as visitors to the country. The whole family experienced "cultural surprise" as we became aware of the superficial differences between American and Egyptian culture.

We were amazed at the variety of dress, from Western suits and ties to fully veiled women. Nonverbal behaviors that might have been insulting in the US were interpreted differently in Egypt. People stood very close together and talked in very loud voices accompanied by waving hands. Were they angry or just enjoying the conversation? Close friends or relatives greeted each other with kisses on both cheeks. Even men kissed each other in the same way. We noticed Egyptians beckoning waiters and even friends by saying "psst" or whistling or clapping.

These differences were proof of the foreign-ness of Egypt and were cause for comments and wonder. We were eager to please the people we met and to cooperate with them, and they also expressed an interest in our backgrounds and experiences. We frequently smiled or nodded to show understanding when, in fact, we hadn't understood the Arabic words, gestures, or accents. Floyd always smiled, ready to accept a handshake or a taste of food from a street vendor. I reminded him that the street food was not properly washed and could cause serious illness. By trying new foods, I think he exemplified "the acceptance of innovations," part of the communications theory that he had taught at Michigan State.

Our neighbors across the hall offered amazing support as we navigated our first months in Cairo. Dr. David Johns was a professor in the political science department, and his wife, Ann, was completing an MA in Teaching English as a Foreign Language. They offered to be on-call for the kids while Floyd and I made our first trip to the city on our own. We wanted to visit the Khan Khalili, a seven-century-old bazaar. We walked five blocks to the local taxi stand and hired the driver of a Fiat. Floyd sat in front while I, appropriately, occupied the back seat by myself. The driver crooned along with the music of a lovelorn female voice.

"*Om Kalthoum*. You must listen! Beautiful," he coached while he fingered the swinging prayer beads and the tiny kewpie doll attached to the rear-view mirror. Both of his hands were frequently off the steering wheel at the same time because he had to gesture out the open window to cars that cut in front of him. It wasn't the typical American raised finger—but all fingers cupped together and waving emphatically. He "hooted" (a term inherited from the Brits) his horn every few seconds in tune with other hooting cars.

We drove down the Corniche, the historic tree-lined highway along the Nile. The traffic was heavy and slow, so we could absorb the mix of modernity and tradition that we saw. Cars and bicycles shared the road with more traditional modes of transport. Camels and donkeys ambled alongside vehicles. Trucks packed with people or sheep were mixed with horse-drawn carts laden with goods or passengers. A cacophony of sounds bombarded our ears: honking horns, shouts from drivers, and the occasional brays of donkeys or grunts from camels. The inner strip of the Corniche was more than a grassy divider; it was a village. A huge banyan tree gave shade to a whole city of occupations: dentists, barbers, food vendors, and car mechanics. Kids who were out of school played in the trees. Two white-uniformed traffic policemen held hands while directing the sea of traffic at cross streets.

In his desire to be a good tour guide, the driver stopped just across from the Khan Khalili market where a large group of people were gathered around ten or twelve men in multi-colored skirts spinning rhythmically to the music of drums and stringed instruments.

"*Darwish*," the driver said. "*Sufi.*"

I knew the term "whirling dervish." This must be what we were watching, a form of active meditation rooted in Sufism or Islamic mysticism. The spectacle of multicolored skirts swirling dramatically mesmerized us. The movements represented a spiritual journey toward divine love and connection with God. A few minutes of amazement ended abruptly when the driver turned to Floyd and rubbed his fingers together.

"*Feloos, min fadlik.*" he said. Money, please.

It was difficult to pull our eyes away from the entrancing, repetitive movement to focus on shopping, but that was the purpose of our trip. We paid the driver, thanked him, and crossed the street to the bazaar and the hawkers of authentic and not-so-authentic wares. The most striking aspect of stepping into the dim, narrow alleyways that went on forever was the mixture of odors. Small pots of incense burned outside the butchers' stalls, attempting to cover the heavy smell of carcasses of water buffalos and lambs hanging from hooks by the doors. Various other scents filled the air, including pungent tobacco (occasionally blended with hashish) from bubbling water pipes, rice and macaroni covered in tomato sauce from a decorated mobile snack counter, spices displayed in open bins, freshly tanned camel and buffalo leather fashioned into poufs and purses, and sporadic hints of sewage. Artisans worked on their crafts, from inlaid boxes to ornate copper trays that took months to detail with tiny chisels and hammers.

I checked my purse to be certain I was clear about the Egyptian coins and paper bills. I had ten smudged and slightly tattered paper bills, Egyptian pounds (LE) or gineih. Also a number of copper-looking coins, called piastres. Each pound was made up of 100 piastres. The approximate exchange rate was $2.30 to one pound.

"Madame, come in. I sell cheap," was the refrain of each shopkeeper.

Floyd preferred to browse the shops and not engage with the hustling shopkeepers. I wanted to try the Arabic I was learning in my class for AUC newcomers, so I convinced him to enter one of the shops with me. Floyd thought he wasn't a good language learner, so he hadn't enrolled in the class. He preferred to stay inside his comfort zone on the campus, where everyone could speak English. I took his arm and guided him into a small, open-fronted shop. The walls were lined with brass pots and intricately designed trays, vases, and candlesticks. I used to enjoy making candles, so I was attracted to the candle holders.

"*Ahlan w'sahlan!*" the owner welcomed us. "I am Mohamed and speak good English. Have coffee while I show you brassware, Madame and Monsieur?"

"*Ahlan bik. Shukran,* Mohamed." I tried out my beginning Arabic to show Mohamed I wasn't just a tourist. We sat down for our very first tiny cups of strong, sweet Turkish coffee, an enticement offered to prospective buyers at many of the artisans' shops. A sip fortified my practice run at bargaining.

"*Eh, da?* Is that candleholder for sale?" I pointed to a decorative piece on the top shelf.

"Yes, Madame. Beautiful antique. Made more than two hundred years ago and only ten pounds."

I gulped a swallow of coffee. Floyd had already finished his.

"Ten pounds? No, that's too much. I wouldn't give more than two pounds for a candlestick," I bravely said.

Floyd fidgeted with his empty cup. My disagreement embarrassed him.

"Two pounds? You insult my worthy goods. But since you are new to the country, I give it away to you at great sacrifice ... only six-fifty."

"I certainly can't spend that much," I said, jumping down to less than half his counteroffer. I really didn't know what I was doing, but I made a stab at a number. Floyd examined the inside of his coffee cup.

"Three pounds."

"*Mish magoul,* Madame!" Impossible! "You insult me and my fine goods."

I noticed the smile in Mohamed's eyes and was ready to finish playing the game. Floyd was mortified and ready to run from the shop.

"Sorry," I said. I put down my cup and started to stand up.

Pretending to be a bit angry, Mohamed replied, "No, no. Wait, Madame. I will sell it for an unbelievable four pounds."

"I'm sorry. I have only three pounds in my purse. I can't spend more than that."

"Three pounds fifty," he muttered, grabbing the candle holder from the shelf. It slipped from his hand and broke in half when it landed on a huge brass pot. The beautiful "brass" candlestick was made of plaster.

"*Ma'alesh,* Madame, wrong candle stick. I show you another one?"

I laughed. He smiled. I thanked him for the coffee and said, "*Ma'alesh,*" no problem.

I caught up with Floyd, who had already left the shop. Hand in hand, we strolled through dozens of other shops and stalls. We watched accomplished artisans working on inlaid boxes, intricate brass trays, mother-of-pearl chess tables, and gold and silver jewelry.

"Madame, Monsieur, come in. I sell cheap," was the repeated invitation to step into another shop. I politely said, "*Shukran,* thanks, but not today."

Floyd agreed.

▲ ▲ ▲

My bargaining skills improved as the weeks went by. Almost every purchasable item in Cairo, from camel saddles to cabbage heads, could be bargained for—except goods sold in the primarily foreign settlements, like Ma'adi or Zamalek, or merchandise in the larger department stores, where the government fixed prices. The government stores conducted business in a no-nonsense manner. The atmosphere in these stores, however, was out of the past: in solid concrete buildings with very little plate glass, no display space, creaking floors smelling of kerosene cleaner, and merchandise reminiscent of the 1950s. The buildings resembled photos I had seen of Soviet Union businesses and possibly were remnants of Nasser's Soviet Union ties. To purchase an item in a government store, you had to choose the article, receive a written slip stating the price, walk to a central cash register and pay, and then take the receipt to another counter, where you received the newspaper-wrapped purchase. However, small shops kept the bazaar alive, where bargaining and display were a rather leisurely social affair. The time consumed in striking a satisfactory bargain could stretch from twenty minutes for a pair of shoes to several weeks of return bargaining sessions for a skillfully engraved brass tray.

▲ ▲ ▲

October 12, 1971

Dear Mama and Daddy,]

Sonja and Missy are enjoying school at CAC. Their subjects include Arabic and French, along with a full American curriculum. The best aspect of CAC is the mixture of students from thirty-four different nations. Sonja is continuing her ballet training in Cairo (and in

*French) from Madame Laurella, a rather stern, demanding ballet
mistress. Missy will begin piano lessons as soon as we can get a
piano carried up the stairs in the apartment building. Troy's favorite
occupations are trying to tame the twenty cats that haunt our
building and riding his tricycle down the road after goat herds.
I've been told that Egyptians feed cats out of respect for Mohammed
the Prophet who, it is said, cut a piece from his cloak rather than
disturb the cat who slept in his lap.*

*Floyd is teaching graduate classes and serves as assistant chair
of the Economics and Political Science Department. The master's
program he's launching is the first of its type in the Middle East.*

*He's delighted with his students who, he says, are among the
brightest and most motivated he has ever taught. Most of them are
women who work in the thriving media industry, including film,
radio, television, and print journalism.*

*I'm taking classes in colloquial Arabic at the university and trying
to practice with the servants, shopkeepers, taxi drivers, and fellow
classmates. I've started writing poetry again and have just been
offered a job next semester at the girls' school, teaching an advanced
English and journalism class to seniors. It should be fun!*

*We've decided to resist buying a car. It would be too expensive
and too dangerous to drive on the crowded, crazy streets of Cairo.
Bicycles work well here in Ma'adi, and the Hungarian-made electric
trains and taxis provide transportation to Cairo and other suburbs.*

*Please write! Airmail takes about ten to twelve days, but surface
mail takes three months!*

Love, Connie, Floyd, and family

▲ ▲ ▲

Mail. I longed for the black metal mailbox next to my front door in
Michigan. I missed the "Good morning" from Jimmy, the postman.
And where was the post office on Main Street? Mail delivery didn't

exist in Cairo—or in Egypt in general. An inefficient government and limited resources led to few services and lost mail. Egyptians primarily collected their mail from government post offices or used institutional channels like AUC for international correspondence. This method ensured that they could maintain communication with friends and family abroad despite the limitations of the local postal system.

A letter to my parents had to be handwritten on blue airmail tissue paper, which was too thin to roll into a typewriter. I would address it to their Denver home and give it to Floyd to deliver to the university mailroom, where it would be added to a pouch to go to AUC's New York office. From there, it would be picked up by the US Postal Service and delivered to my mom and dad. When my parents sent us a letter, they would address it to the AUC office in New York, which would send it in an airmail pouch to Cairo. Once we made friends in the community, it was possible, occasionally, to ask a person traveling to the States to mail a letter to family and friends.

I didn't even think about taking photos at this stage in our adjustment to Cairo, but I wished later for an easy way to send photos home to the States. Photos could not be sent in airmail stationery envelopes. Our Brownie camera was limited in quality, film development was expensive, and strong prohibitions were in place against photographing government buildings, streets, signs, and who knew what else.

After a few months, we managed to send an occasional black and white photo of the children with friends who were going to the States, where they could mail them to Denver. Photo opportunities were just a few feet away from our apartment building. Writing became my way of preserving these intriguing scenes and the fascinating Egyptians we met on our doorstep.

▲ ▲ ▲

"Oh, Who Are the People in Our Neighborhood, the People That We Meet Each Day?" was one of Troy's favorite songs. When we left the US, *Sesame Street* was just becoming popular. Although our present Ma'adi neighbors were a far cry from the mailman, policeman, and grocer on Sesame Street, they were far more interesting. The Egg Lady was one of the most attractive people who came to the apartments.

Each morning, she glided up the winding stairs to our third floor apartment carrying on her head a reed basket of tiny hens' eggs. A long-sleeved black melaya almost covered her sandaled feet. Bracelets and beads, some in turquoise blue to keep away the evil eye, provided bright relief from her somber outfit.

The Egg Lady's children sat patiently in the dust of the street while she bargained with customers. One of them, a little girl of four or five, sometimes crumbled up a small ball of beans from her *ful* sandwich to feed her four-month-old brother. When the Egg Lady lifted the basket to her head to make the return trip down the stairs, her *melaya* revealed a small tattooed blue cross on her wrist, a symbol of her Coptic Orthodox Christian religion. Her delicate features and large almond eyes resembled the bas-relief figures on the walls of ancient temples of the Pharisees. The Copts, who numbered almost three million in Egypt in the 1970's, were considered descendants of Pharaonic Egyptians.

The Flute Man was another colorful character in the neighborhood. Our children could hear him coming from at least a kilometer away, playing the loudest flute in his collection as he soft-shoed down the road. This pied-piper vendor was always followed by an entourage of children who loved his music but couldn't afford to buy the bamboo flutes, which ranged from twenty *piastres* to two pounds. The basket on his back was filled with every size and shape of horn, most of them too difficult for the untrained person to play.

Aside from the Flute Man, one of the most melodious neighbors we had was the Junk Man, also known as the Rag Picker.

"*Roba bekieh, be-kieh,*" he sang as he announced his collection. The Junk Man picked up empty bottles, old newspapers, rags discarded from street sweepers, tattered shoes, and anything else that was used and unwanted. He sold his junk to someone who could wear it, burn it, or re-use it. Most Egyptians had never heard the word "recycle" but had been doing it for centuries. The Junk Man's discarded soft drink bottles, for example, were melted down and shaped into lovely vases, glasses, and water carafes. Tourists shopped for this distinctive blue or amber Mousky glass as a special souvenir of Cairo.

"Today, lady—for you, my friend—a very special price," was the daily greeting of the Basket Man as he brought his donkey cart up to the apartment house gate. His cart was filled with colorful reed baskets of all shapes, from the tiniest two-inch ring box to a two-foot-tall laundry basket, which I purchased. The Basket Man's creations originated from the village of Tunis in Fayoum. They were made of a variety of materials: palm leaves, reeds, and papyrus stalks.

A young boy on a bicycle brought freshly baked loaves of *aish shami,* a plump type of Syrian pita bread, early in the morning, piled precariously high in a basket on his head. He would stop at the apartment house to make sales to the cooks, who would briefly singe individual pieces over the gas flame on their stoves to sterilize them, in case the bread had toppled onto the dirt road and returned to the basket.

Next came the fruit and vegetable cart. An old man who could barely walk would plod along, leading his donkey and cart to each house along the street. The cart overflowed with tomatoes, cabbage heads, squash, lemons, pomegranates, mangoes, oranges, and more. He announced his produce by shouting greetings of the day, "*Saeeda! Saeeda! Saeeda!*" to his customers.

The Trash Man

"Ro-ba-bekia! Ro-ba-bekia!"
sung in tenor voice
with vibrato choice
Is it opera? Russian folk music?

Syncopated scraps
accompanied by squeals
of wooden cart wheels
the Junk Man's chorus.

An old shoe will do,
rags, bags, scraps of tin,
trash is my treasure
"Ro-ba-bekia! Ro-ba-bekia!"

The Street Sweeper

He rises in the dawn
when the muezzin calls
and brushing the dust
from his sand-hued clothes
he gropes for the tool
of his toil and his trade
smooth-handled from fingers
that grip its shaft.

No tycoon knows business
better than he
The street is his office
there he predicts
the rise of each khamseen
the fall of each leaf
His stock is in dung heaps
piled by the road.

His shares are the piastres
lost by schoolboys
the papers and bottles
thrown in the dirt,
all earned with each whisk
and scrape of his broom
the dividend of his sweat and strain.

3

The Honeymoon Is Over

IT WAS SUNDAY, October 17. Our bag of new experiences was packed so full we couldn't add one new item. It was time to sort through all we had seen, heard, smelled, and tasted in the almost five weeks since we had arrived at Cairo International Airport: sightseeing tours, moving to an apartment, starting school and university, using taxis and trains, eating new foods, and trying to learn enough Arabic to negotiate our daily routines. My brain tried to process this sensory overload as I sat on the small balcony of our third-floor apartment, contemplating what I would write in my weekly letter home. *Maghrib,* the sunset prayer time, sounded from the minaret of a nearby mosque, followed by the echoes of other mosques in the distance.

All my previous letters had been filled with the excitement of new experiences in an amazing city. Today, I was filled with home-sickness, a longing for the familiar parts of our daily US routine. I never appreciated having a car to drive wherever I wanted. The decision not to buy a car was based on the danger of driving in Cairo traffic and the cost of purchasing a vehicle. This meant we had to use public transportation, either train or taxi, for trips outside of Ma'adi. However, after one trip on the second-class train with Floyd, I decided it wasn't for me or for the family in general. It was too crowded, and too many unwanted male hands touched me.

Walking was a great way, although slow, of getting around Ma'adi. It was such a quiet, safe town. Everyone was helpful and concerned about the children. On Sonja and Missy's first walk home alone from school, a German woman greeted them and asked if they were finding their way all right. She offered to walk with them to be sure they arrived at the apartment house.

Crime, other than theft of a tangerine from a tree or a shirt from a clothesline, seemed to be nonexistent here and, basically, in Cairo. No one was allowed to own a gun except for special police units and the army. Any reported crime or suspicion of a crime was punished severely, usually preceded by a beating until confession, I was told. This was a horrible fact of life for any Egyptian but an assurance of safety for an expatriate family.

Sonja and Missy felt safe walking to school but anxiously waited for our shipment of their bicycles from the port at Alexandria so they could cycle to CAC. I planned to buy a bicycle from Ayyad's shop with a seat for Troy on the back.

High on the list of other things we missed were familiar foods: pasteurized cows' milk (Floyd used to drink several glasses a day), peanut butter, Kool-Aid, cereals like Raisin Bran and Grape Nuts (instead of those only-available Corn Flakes), sandwich bread, mayonnaise, and beef roast.

I missed a department store like K-Mart, where we could have purchased all the things we didn't bring with us in one place: flashlights, soft pillows, and scissors. We envied the company-employed families who brought all their furniture and possessions with them in addition to some of them having the "privileges" of American canned goods, as well as turkeys and hams for the holidays. University employees lived only on the local economy.

What we longed for the most was the easy ability to communicate with friends and family. The desert island of our isolation was a shock. We missed calling parents and friends long distance, which now required a telephone operator, clearance to prove we weren't spies, planning for the eight-hour time difference, and a phone system that provided clarity of communication rather than static. In the 1970's, there were no cell phones and no text messages. There were no FaceTime nor Zoom calls. We couldn't fly home to Denver for a week or drive or take a train to spend holidays with families.

Even though animals surrounded us, we missed our beloved pets: Taffy, the corgi, and Tiger, the cat that made four moves with us, plus Robin, our young Siamese kitten. Troy had already adopted one of the many kittens that haunted the back doorsteps of the apartment. We called her Hatshepsut, after the Egyptian queen, or Patches for short.

What did the absence of all these familiar parts of our lives do to our adjustment? It forced us to settle in. There was no other alternative.

Our task right now was to substitute new things for those we lacked. The children and I became acquainted with Ma'adi taxi drivers, practiced Arabic directions to our house, and got used to waiting patiently for their arrival. Floyd continued riding the second-class train with buddies from the university because it provided quick transportation and an opportunity to learn about Egyptian society and culture.

Instead of calling home, I wrote weekly letters to my parents, which were sent through an AUC pouch to its New York office or tucked into the baggage of new friends who traveled to the States and would mail the letters there. My mom was a great letter writer, so we appreciated the frequent communication, which was read to all at the dinner table.

Salim was learning about the foods we missed and often fixing us fresh-squeezed orange juice for breakfast, boiled (and cooled) cows' milk when it was available, freshly-baked *aish shami* bread, home-made mayonnaise, and some delicious Egyptian dishes: *ta'amiya,* fava beans with tomato, onions and tahini; *koshari,* a spicy favorite of locals served over rice, and roast chicken *shwarma* sandwiches. It would take the kids a while to warm up to these, but at least they tasted them. Salim gave peanut butter a try, but it was too time-consuming and difficult to make without a mixer of some kind.

▲ ▲ ▲

I postponed writing my letter and left the balcony. Maybe tomorrow. Salim didn't work on Fridays, so I needed to fix a light supper. There were no leftovers in the refrigerator. They seemed to disappear quickly. I prepared some scrambled eggs and toasted some pita bread over the gas flame on the stove, plus the usual array of bananas, olives, and well-washed grapes. I opened the balcony doors, hoping for a cool breeze) while we ate. We could hear a duet of sounds: the evening chants from the Coptic seminary nearby and the discordant screeches of fruit bats feeding on the fig trees that lined our street.

Floyd's stomach was bothering him, so he skipped our supper and went to the bedroom to lie down.

The lights in the apartment house flickered on and off, as they sometimes did, so the evening routine of Sonja reading one of the many books she had checked out from the CAC Library and Missy playing with her Barbie dolls was cut short, and everyone went to bed early. I told Troy a bedtime story and tucked him in. When I went to our bedroom to get ready for bed, I found Floyd shivering and doubled up under the spread.

"My stomach hurts so much. It feels like contractions, like it must feel to have a baby," he said as he struggled to sit up on the side of the bed.

I helped him to the bathroom. Diarrhea and vomiting took over immediately. After a violent bout of retching, the apartment lights went on and off again. In the dark of the bathroom, I tried to clean him up and get him back to bed. I wiped his sweaty forehead with a cool washcloth and laid a towel around his chest as he lay back on the pillow. He couldn't keep down sips of water or the anti-diarrhea meds I had located in a bedside drawer. The vomiting and diarrhea just wouldn't stop. This was more than just the occasional bout of gyppy tummy we had experienced since we arrived.

During our courtship and marriage, Floyd had been through several illnesses and hospitalizations, starting with his third occurrence of rheumatic fever, followed by exploratory stomach surgery for a blood clot, all while we were in the first throes of love as seniors in high school. He also followed a daily penicillin regimen throughout college to prevent the return of rheumatic fever. The pressure of grad school added occasional migraines and the possibility of an ulcer. I was always on the alert when he felt unwell and responded with medical help and reminders of medication routines. Good medical help was available in each of the places we had lived.

But what to do now? I fumbled through the bedside drawers and located the booklet of AUC telephone numbers but couldn't read it in the dark. Flashlights hadn't been on our list of necessities. My mind raced over the options: Who can I ask for help? Would a doctor come to the house? If we had to go to the hospital, how would we get there? None of the people I knew here in the apartment house had cars. Could we call a taxi? What hospital would we go to?

I told Floyd I was going across the hall to ask for help from David and Ann, new acquaintances who had been at AUC for more than a year. They should know what to do. They responded immediately and helped me call Dr. Frank Blanning, the dean of the AUC faculty and a nearby resident here in Ma'adi.

The rest of that night's horrific story is best told by a reporter for The Caravan, the AUC student newspaper, dated November 3, 1972. I discovered this article written in Arabic and translated into English in the AUC archives as I drafted Ma'alesh all these years later. (Note: The language mistakes of the student reporter are not corrected.)

▲ ▲ ▲

Shoemaker Recuperating After Attack of Gastritis

"Dr. Floyd Shoemaker, head of the university's new journalism program, is recuperating at his home in Ma'adi from a near fatal stom-

ach infection 17 October that hospitalized him for eight days. He is expected to return to work this week. Dr. Shoemaker was stricken with cramps, vomiting and diarrhea about 11 p.m. after a Sunday at his home at 20 Rd. 15. He said he tried to tough it out until morning but fearing collapse from loss of blood and dehydration, he asked his wife, Connie, at 5 a.m. to get a doctor. Mrs. Shoemaker called Dr. Frank W. Blanning, Dean of Faculty and a Ma'adi neighbor, who summoned Dr. Salem of Ma'adi. Dr. Salem ordered immediate hospitalization.

"By this time, the 38-year-old professor and author, was suffering from lack of consciousness and unable to focus his eyes. Mr. Blanning drove him to Abbassi, to a maternity hospital run by Italian nuns near Malek Al-Saleh railroad station. He lost his way several times in the unfamiliar streets. There was further delay at the hospital before Dr. Shoemaker was admitted. He was placed in a maternity room, all other rooms being occupied. Dr. Nabil Sheta, the university physician, who had been alerted by Mr. Blanning, arrived at the hospital, ordered Dr. Shoemaker placed on the critical list for two days with sharply lowered blood pressure and a weak and irregular pulse. "Severe stomach infection" was Dr. Sheta's diagnosis. It was complicated by a peptic ulcer which Dr. Shoemaker had suffered before coming to Egypt. Dr. Sheta said if it had not been for Dr. Shoemaker's naturally strong constitution, he might not have survived.

"He ordered Dr. Shoemaker to rest at home for 14 days after his discharge from the hospital on Monday, 25 October.

During his first three days in the hospital, Dr. Shoemaker took no food but lived on 30 injections of glucose in addition to salt fluids and fresh blood. His weight dropped while in the hospital from 167 to 142, a loss of 25 pounds...."

▲ ▲ ▲

My additions to the newspaper story are more personal. Dean Blanning and our neighbor David managed to get Floyd down the stairs and into the back seat of the car, where I held him upright. I didn't have anything to wrap around him to protect the seat of the car except a small rug from the apartment. An Egyptian doctor who Dr. Blanning knew had suggested the Italian hospital, but it was in an area that was unfamiliar to the dean, who was also new to Cairo. It took what seemed like hours to locate the hospital. Meanwhile, Floyd was semi-conscious and moaning. I wrapped my arms around him and kept talking to him.

When we got to the Italian hospital at one a.m., we discovered it was a "lying in" hospital for mothers giving birth. Would they be able to treat Floyd here? All the doors were locked. Dr. Blanning kept ringing the hanging bell until two cleaning men came out. There was no gurney or stretcher, just the two men who put their cleaning rags over their shoulders. One of the men took Floyd's shoulders and the other his legs, and they carried him into the hospital. I was shocked and speechless. I have no memory of going in with him, meeting a doctor, or anything else. All I remember is getting back to the apartment hours later.

Dean Blanning called me the next morning to tell me Floyd was receiving treatment and responding well. I visited the Italian hospital daily, taking a taxi from Ma'adi, usually accompanied by the kids or by Ann. Floyd looked pale and gaunt but always responded positively with his cheerful "thank you" and "I'm OK."

As the oldest of four boys during the Depression, he was taught to work hard next to his father in jobs ranging from ranch hand to house painter. There was no time to complain or be ill when you had a family of five to feed.

The hospital had a staff of Italian nuns who spoke no English but were kind and solicitous when we came to visit. One of the nuns proudly took me by the arm and guided me to the nursery so I could look at the babies in their bassinets. I couldn't believe they would allow me to stand in front of a bassinet with no barriers between the newborns and me. One of them even asked if I would like to hold a baby. I smiled and said, "No, thank you."

Toward the end of his stay, Floyd was allowed to begin eating. I assumed he would have food from the hospital kitchen but soon found out that families were supposed to supply food for the patients. Salim prepared some mild, soft foods for me to take. On one of the visits, I put some cookies wrapped in a napkin onto Floyd's bedside table near an open window. It wasn't long until a cat jumped into the window sill and knocked a cookie off the plate onto the street below.

In my conversations with Ma'adi acquaintances after Floyd was recuperating at home, the diagnosis of severe gastritis was questioned. A neighbor, an American doctor working with NAMRU (Naval Medical Research Unit) suggested that Floyd had much more than simple gastritis. He said the symptoms fit a disease that was prevalent in Cairo at the time: cholera. The entire family had had cholera vaccinations before we came and were told this preventive vaccine would be necessary every six months. Our neighbor told us it was still possible to contract cholera even after vaccination, particularly in areas like Egypt where it was endemic or during an outbreak. Also, he said some individuals may not respond adequately to the vaccine, depending on their individual immune systems.

I guessed that AUC did not want to announce a diagnosis of cholera. It would have been discomforting news for foreign faculty and their families. We had understood that cholera was a threat—hence, the required inoculations—but we didn't realize how prevalent the disease was. My later research revealed that Egypt was affected by the seventh cholera pandemic, which was especially deadly in developing countries, during the '60s and '70s. These countries shared challenges related to water treatment, sanitation infrastructure, and healthcare access.

▲ ▲ ▲

We happily brought Floyd home on October 25, just six weeks after our arrival in Cairo. It was also only three days before the beginning of Ramadan, the month-long period of fasting required by Islam. In a reversal of Ramadan requirements, Floyd had already finished his hospital fast and needed to build up his strength by eating small portions of bland food. As we furthered our understanding of Egypt and its people, we recognized the importance of gaining a deeper knowledge of Islam, the religion practiced by eighty-six percent of the population.

Ramadan is one of the most important requirements of Islam, one of its Five Pillars. It is the ninth month of the Islamic calendar, a lunar calendar of twelve months in a year of 354 or 355 days, as opposed to the Gregorian calendar, which is based on a complete orbit of the Earth around the sun. The Islamic calendar is used primarily to determine proper days for holidays and rituals.

During Ramadan, all healthy adult Muslims are required to abstain from food, drink, and sensual pleasures from dawn until sunset. This practice is ordained in the Holy Qur'an, the religious text of Islam. The month focuses on deep personal worship aimed at increasing a Muslim's perception of God and their sensitivity to the sufferings of the poor. It also commemorates the month when the Qur'an was first revealed to the Prophet Muhammad.

Ramadan is marked by increased prayer times and ends with the celebration of Eid al-Fitr, a festive occasion that includes family reunions and the exchange of gifts, particularly for children. This is a day to give a designated amount of money to the poor and needy, a practice called Zakat al-Fitr. The amount is based on local food prices and economic conditions.

On the first day of this holy month, Salim came out of the kitchen, smiling and ready to teach me.

"Ramadan very good, *Ma sha Allah!*" as God has willed. "Not good for Salim. Salim no eat." He laughed and rubbed his stomach.

"I hope it's a good Ramadan, with Allah's blessings, Salim."

"Madame must say '*Ramadan Kareem* now. Then at end of Ramadan, say *Eid Mubarak*."

I repeated the phrases, noticing they resembled our wishes for a Merry Christmas and a Happy New Year, but they used the new year in a religious context. Now, Muslims wished for a month filled with Allah's blessings. On the feast day at the end of Ramadan, they congratulated each other on the successful completion of the fasting month and wished for a joyful and blessed Eid celebration.

We saw Ramadan in action at the apartment house and on our taxi rides. Salim and the other male cooks and *suffragis* followed their usual prayer times but with more fervor. They stopped their tasks and gathered to pray in the courtyard of the building. Women servants prayed quietly in their kitchens. During the usual prayer times in downtown Cairo, men hurried to the mosques or joined other worshippers in the streets, who gathered to perform their prayers. Hundreds of men spilled onto sidewalks or any spot that had room for them to kneel on their prayer rugs. Added to the five prayer times, they spent more time reading the Qur'an and offering special prayers at the mosques to be closer to Allah.

We noticed a slower, more serious attitude in the populace. Energy levels were lower, arguments were not as loud, and grumpiness was more prevalent. After sundown and prayers, the fast was broken by *iftar,* the meal that Muslims eat to break their fast at sunset during Ramadan. Dates and water or milk were often eaten before dinner itself. Everyone was also allowed to snack and hydrate between dusk and dawn. Older people slept after the meal, but the younger population stayed up most of the night playing games, visiting, and enjoying family and friends.

Ten years later, I shared this first Ramadan experience with the Saudi and Kuwaiti students who were late or didn't show up for classes at the ESL program I directed in Denver. They told me they had played cards through the night and had pizza right before sunrise when fasting began. Then, they went to bed instead of coming to class. The only difference here was the pizza.

Troy was the first family member to participate in the daily Ramadan schedule. He disappeared from the apartment just before bedtime on the first day of fasting. Sonja went downstairs to look for him and found him happily sitting next to Salim on the veranda with all the other cooks and *suffragis*. He was eating a big slice of watermelon and trying to balance a plate of *kubsa,* a chicken and rice dish; on his knees. Troy was breaking the fast even though he hadn't fasted.

Floyd was given a week to recuperate at home before he went back to his classes. Luckily for his limited energy, during Ramadan, lectures were shortened from ninety minutes to just an hour and were offered in midday instead of mid-afternoon—when naps were usually the order of the day. The schedule at CAC stayed the same, from 9am to 3pm, because the students represented many different cultures and religions.

Since I was basically a housewife and mom at this point, my schedule didn't change. However, I did try to fast, so I could have a taste, so to speak, of what it would be like to be an observant Muslim. It only lasted two days, mainly because of the no-water prohibition during the day.

Temperatures in October were in the nineties, and there was no air conditioning inside. In addition, I had to bicycle Troy to his play-group and walk outdoors. On the third day, I became dehydrated and dizzy. My fasting attempt was finished, but my compassion for those fasting had increased.

The month of Ramadan fasting ended the day after the new moon was seen at dawn. It was Eid-al-Fitr, the Festival of Break-ing the Fast. Firecrackers announced a celebration like no other. It was reminiscent of bits of American Halloween, Easter, and Thanksgiving, all put together. Children carried lanterns door-to-door begging for treats, prayers gave thanks for the strength Allah had imparted to everyone during the fasting, and children received presents and new clothes. Young girls decorated their hands with henna. Family members traveled from far and wide to be together, and women were often given small gifts to mark the occasion by their loved ones. Lunch became the main meal for families on this day.

▲ ▲ ▲

As our family walked down the decorated main road of shops in Ma'adi, we could smell spiced rice, fish, and meat. It seemed as if every resident of our suburb was out on the street. All schools, government workplaces, and colleges were closed during this time. All along the Corniche, which was decorated and lit up with lanterns, mobile carnivals, performers, and storytellers entertained the crowds with traditional folktales. Although we were just observers, the *Eid* celebration lifted our spirits and gave us insight into the joyful and fun-loving Egyptians.

▲ ▲ ▲

We had completed ten eventful weeks of life in Cairo. We were more than visitors. And we needed to adapt to life in this fascinating and stressful city. Like many minority groups in a new culture, we circled the wagons with friends to protect ourselves as we crossed the prairie of a new culture.

AUC recognized the difficulties of cultural adaptation and did its best to establish a support system that included cultural and historical trips and tours, Arabic language classes, assistance with housing, and household help. The apartment complex provided us with a community of new and experienced faculty to commiserate with and guide us. The American community in Ma'adi and at CAC also supported newcomers with activities, interest groups of everything from square dancing to community theater, and an essential telephone book of Ma'adi expats. We even received a book of recipes and a guide on where to buy special ingredients and other essentials.

Our new friends included our across-the-hall apartment mates: David and Ann—who had come to our aid during Floyd's cholera crisis—three-year-old Timmy, and five-year-old Beth. In their second year of tenure at the university, they had a wealth of practical knowledge. We enjoyed the friendship of Bill and Anne Marie Harrison, plus Justin, Troy's buddy in Big Wheel maneuvers, and Madoline, Justin's younger sibling. Bill was a Ford Foundation executive and later became an administrator at AUC. I also made friends with the CAC teachers and some of the oil company wives, a close-knit group posted frequently to other Middle Eastern installations that required them to start their lives repeatedly in new cultures and environments. They gave emotional and social support to each other. I tried to take advantage of all the university offered in addition to the most important tasks: encouraging Sonja and Missy in their adjustment and school activities, as well as taking care of Troy and supporting Floyd's well-being, all necessary for the family to successfully embark on our new venture.

What Am I Doing Here?

Plump Gerber babies cooing
out of glossy color ads.
Enriched milk and diet fads
vitamins and kitchen-tested cakes.
This is my world.

Sidestepping filth that runs
between the cobblestones
where a babe with flies
for nose and eyes
sits wrapped in rags of hunger.
I wonder,
What am I doing here?

4

Life Is the River

ALHAMDULILLAH! THANKS BE to God! Floyd was feeling much better after recuperating from cholera at home for several weeks. He was twenty pounds thinner but slowly gaining some weight. Tutoring from more experienced cooks in the building had encouraged Salim to add some more appealing dishes to his repertoire, and Floyd's appetite was improving. He had enough energy to sign us up for AUC's trip up the Nile, an annual fall event for new faculty and their spouses. Children weren't included, so we would have to arrange for David, Ann, and Salim to take care of Sonja, Missy, and Troy.

At almost eleven years old, Sonja was also a helpful and wise big sister to Troy. I realized that we already had a strong support system right here in the building, but I was still worried about leaving the kids. We had never done this in the States with all three kids for more than a few hours with a babysitter. In my usual two a.m. ponderings, I considered encouraging Floyd to go by himself. I could be here with the kids and unpack the full bag of daily concerns I needed to address. However, Floyd dismissed my worries about the trip and trusted our arrangements for the children's care. He also was unusually candid about his own health.

"I'd feel much better if you were with me," he said.

It was a done deal. We signed up for the ten-day trip and made caregiving preparations. After all, it was a once-in-a-lifetime opportunity to learn more about this complex and amazing country.

▲ ▲ ▲

Along with about one hundred university faculty and assorted spouses, we boarded the *Isis* riverboat embarking on a journey up the Nile from Cairo to Aswan. Why do we say "up the Nile"? We literally traveled toward the source of the river located in East Africa. "Down the Nile" would imply traveling toward Alexandria, its mouth in the Mediterranean.

Isis, the name of our riverboat, reminded me of a favorite Denver theater from my childhood, but then I didn't know I'd be embarking on a vessel named for the major goddess in ancient Egyptian history, the queen to King Osiris. The boat was a luxurious diesel-powered vessel with well-appointed cabins, dining areas, lounges, and outdoor deck spaces. We boarded near the hotel district and sailed south, passing through a series of villages and towns that each held their own historical significance and cultural heritage.

It was a magical trip floating back in time thousands of years. We could see *fellahin*, Egyptian peasants, encouraging their water buffalos to plod in a circle powering a crank attached to an Archimedes screw, drawing water from the Nile to irrigate their crops. Women washed clothes in shallow waters. Men unmoored their *feluccas*, the boats used by the Egyptians since the beginning of their civilization, to travel to the next village or to fish in the river. Young boys splashed and bathed in the water. Everyone waved as we passed by.

Zahi Hawass was our tour guide for the Nile trip. His briefings along the way were knowledgeable, authoritative and humorous. He had recently completed a postgraduate course in Egyptology at Cairo University. We didn't know then that he would become a famous Egyptologist and the Minister of Antiquities. He later won a Fulbright grant and a place in the PhD program at the University of Pennsylvania. In 1987, he completed his PhD and returned to Egypt.

Zahi, as he asked to be called, was particularly interested in one of the first sites we passed, Hermopolis, a once thriving city that worshipped Thoth—the god of wisdom, writing, and magic. The ancient Egyptians believed this was where creation began. The city played a crucial role in religious and cultural life and was a center of learning and scholarship. Zahi would later become the primary excavator of this site.

The boat docked briefly at Tel el Amarna, the site of the ancient city of Akhetaten, established in approximately 1348 BCE. This city was dedicated to the worship of the sun god Aten, leading to a shift in religious practices toward the worship of a single deity. Recent excavations had revealed an open-air temple and royal residences with elaborate mudbrick walls and decorated interiors.

Hathor, the goddess of love and joy, greeted us the next day as we passed by the temples at Abydos and Dendera. Hathor was considered a nurturing mother figure and a protector of women during childbirth. The rituals performed here were believed to ensure fertility and health for both mothers and their children.

Learning about these ancient rituals made me realize how comforting it is to participate in a ritual in a place of worship or just in daily life. I could see that part of our adjustment in Cairo was following old rituals, like bedtime stories, dinner time sharing of daily events, and participating in a church community. These practices assured us of a positive transition to a new environment. New rituals? I still struggled with these.

The highlight of our trip was Luxor, the ancient city of Thebes. We docked and spent the night on the boat. The next morning, we joined Zahi to explore the royal burial grounds of the Valley of the Kings and the Valley of the Queens.

The Valley of the Kings contains more than sixty elaborate rock-cut tombs, including those of famous rulers such as Tutankhamun, Seti I, and Ramses II. The rugged terrain and steep cliffs provided a natural barrier that helped conceal these royal burials from tomb robbers. However, they weren't well-hidden enough to prevent their robbery shortly after they were sealed. Archaeological evidence suggests that many treasures were looted even before ancient records documented their existence.

Luckily, some tombs, like that of Tutankhamun, remained largely intact until their discovery in modern times. We planned to enter King Tut's tomb, but preservation concerns and potential damage from heavy foot traffic prevented this. My claustrophobia said that was preferable. Instead of allowing tourists inside, a replica of the burial chamber provided us with an opportunity to experience the tomb without causing further harm to the original site.

After a full day of walking, Floyd and I ate dinner in the Luxor Hotel's dining room and then hired a horse-drawn carriage to take us on a slow ride through the tree-lined streets. What a lovely city! As night fell, streetlamps illuminated narrow streets, where locals gathered to socialize or play *shahmat*, Egyptian chess. We could hear traditional music played on the strings of an *oud* and a flute wafting through the air from a nearby cafe. How pleasant it was to hold hands and drink in the romantic atmosphere, a dream from our first days in Egypt.

The next day we visited Karnak, just north of Luxor. Karnak was the monumental city of Thebes. It was hard to fathom that the huge pillars, chapels and temples dated as far back as 1,971 years before Christ (BCE). The Karnak Temple is one of the largest religious buildings in the world. It was dedicated to a triad of gods: Amun, Mut, and Khonsu.

Our boat was headed toward Aswan, our final destination. We passed by Edfu, home to one of the best-preserved temples in Egypt, dedicated to Horus. I had never imagined crocodiles in the Nile, but the next village, Kom Ombo, had a unique double temple dedicated to Sobek, the crocodile god, and Horus, the god of war and the sky.

The most amazing and controversial site of our trip was Aswan, located on the east bank of the Nile. As we approached the city, we could see lush green islands and a few remaining Nubian villages. The reconstruction work on the Temple of Philae on Agilkia Island, about five hundred meters north of its original site on Philae Island, was an amazing site. The entire temple was moved to protect it from the rising waters of Lake Nasser. The temple blocks were disassembled, labeled, and recorded individually, so it could be reassembled accurately at its new location.

The next day featured a visit to the new Aswan High Dam. Floyd was very tired at this point, so we opted out of the trip, but Zahi's lecture at breakfast impressed us. We found out the dam was completed just before we arrived in Cairo. Zahi pointed out the negative and the positive aspects of this huge project. It was considered a monumental engineering achievement that controlled the Nile's flooding, generated hydroelectric power, and improved irrigation for agriculture. It created Lake Nasser, one of the world's largest artificial lakes. The dam was built with significant expertise from the Soviet Union, the reason we saw so many Russians in Cairo.

Zahi filled us in on the history of the dam. Its construction began in 1960 and was completed in 1970, just a year before we arrived in Egypt. Unfortunately, more than one hundred thousand people, primarily from Nubian communities along the river, were forced to leave their ancestral homes, particularly those located in areas that would be submerged by Lake Nasser, which had formed behind the dam. Yet, the relocation of thousands of people seemed to be of little concern in exchange for generating electricity for all of Egypt.

Zahi was careful to avoid any political commentary, but we got the factual background later from an American journalist who was traveling with us. Initially, both the United States and Britain offered financial support for the dam, proposing a $270 million loan. However, this offer was withdrawn in 1956 after Egypt signed a secret arms deal with the Soviet Union. In response to losing Western funding, Nasser nationalized the British- and French-owned Suez Canal to use its toll revenues to finance the dam. This act led to the Suez Crisis of 1956 but ultimately left Egypt in control of the canal. With tensions between Egypt and Western powers escalating, Nasser turned to the Soviet Union for assistance in the shape of significant loans and technical expertise for constructing the Aswan High Dam.

Our cook, Salim, had told me he was a *Sudani,* a Nubian, so I was particularly interested in the history of his people. The Nubians originated from the early Black inhabitants of the central Nile Valley, one of the earliest cradles of civilization. They speak Nubian languages as their mother tongue and Arabic as a second language. Historically, while the Nubians were citizens of Egypt at the time of the Aswan Dam's construction, they had little influence over decisions regarding their displacement and suffered severely because of this major infrastructure project. They were forcibly relocated to new settlements away from their traditional lands. The relocation process was often poorly managed. Many Nubians faced inadequate compensation and insufficient infrastructure in their new homes. This disruption in their lives not only affected their livelihoods but also threatened their cultural heritage and community cohesion.

Salim had come to Cairo as part of the displaced families from this area. When we told him we were going to see the Aswan dam, he said, "*Ana Sudani.*" I am Sudanese. "Big lake, no home, no work. Family leave and come here."

In addition to human displacement, important archaeological sites, like the Temple of Philae, were also submerged under Lake Nasser. The silt that used to be deposited by flooding led to decreased soil fertility in farming areas downstream, which had previously led to the export of agricultural products and good fishing that provided food for everyone.

While most of our tour group went on to view the High Dam, Floyd was up for a leisurely stroll on Kitchener's Island to see the tropical gardens established by Lord Horatio Kitchener, who was Consul-General in Egypt during the British occupation. He was given the island and took on the task of transforming it into a botanical paradise. He imported exotic trees and plants from various regions, particularly India and Malaysia, to create lush gardens.

We enjoyed the beauty of the gardens but realized there was a dark history of British repression behind the lovely flowers and trees. The period from 1882 until Egypt gained nominal independence in 1922 was marked by political unrest, economic exploitation, and social inequality. The occupation changed the direction of Egypt's economy toward serving British needs, such as boosting cotton production for British industries. They also took control of the Suez Canal, giving them strategic military positioning and used Egypt's treasury to serve their own economic interests rather than benefiting Egyptians.

We joined our AUC friends for a final dinner in the Luxor Hotel before boarding the Isis to return to Luxor, where we caught an overnight train back to Cairo. As we looked out the window at the fast-moving landscape, we struggled to wrap our minds around the centuries of history preserved in the sites we had visited. We were beginning to see the impact of this rich cultural heritage in the lives of present-day Egyptians. My near-sighted focus on everyday irritations was broadening into an admiration for the true character of the people. A sense of pride was part of this character, pride that led to preserving historical traditions and maintaining connections to ancient roots. The annual influx of tourists visiting the historical sites reinforced the connection to Egyptian heritage. This economic reliance on ancient history influenced how present-day Egyptians viewed their past—not just something to be preserved but also as an essential part of their economic future.

Along with the strength of their Islamic beliefs, many present-day Egyptians still held religious beliefs that reflected their ancient reverence for the cycles of the Nile, such as the celebration of spring, the *Shem el Nessim* holiday we would enjoy at Easter. The legacy of ancient Egypt also played a crucial role in shaping the national identity. Symbols from ancient Egypt were prevalent in modern culture—from art to architecture—and contributed to a unique sense of belonging among the people. Egypt's long history strongly influenced its culture, values, and economy.

Our Nile journey brought into sharper focus the contrast between American and Egyptian cultures. The United States is such a young nation, with a history spanning just a few centuries. American culture is characterized by innovation, progress, and change. We pride ourselves on embracing new ideas and technologies. Offering the knowledge of ways to communicate new ideas and technologies with the goal of acceptance by the Egyptian people—in other words, the communication of innovations in a developing country—challenged Floyd. This acceptance of new ideas had to build upon Egypt's rich cultural heritage, not destroy it.

Velvet Eyes

Velvet eyes of Hatshepsut
arched with kohl
are born again
and mouths that kissed in ecstasy
shadowed by the Kings' Valley
are born again
and coupled bodies in a barge
on the crocodiled Nile
are born again
and lovers' pledges
sealed eternally in golden tombs
are born again
and they're returning
with the names
of your sons and daughters.

5

The Turkey Trot

IT WAS NOVEMBER 1971. When we lived in the States, no matter where we pursued Floyd's degrees, we had always traveled home to Denver for the holidays. It was a tradition to have turkey dinner at Grandma and Grandad Shoemaker's house, visit Grandma and Grandad Johnson, my parents, for Christmas goodies and gift opening, and then drop in on the Great Grandparents Grondahl, who were in their eighties and lived in Longmont, Colorado. This would be our first Thanksgiving and Christmas holidays celebrated without our extended family.

Here in Cairo, Thanksgiving, Christmas, and birthdays were fast approaching. I became involved in the American community by writing a monthly newsletter, the *Ma'adi Messenger*, sponsored by the American Women's Organization and distributed to the English-speaking community. This made me a target of other requests and volunteer efforts. An annual Thanksgiving dinner at CAC required multiple volunteers. My newly honed bargaining skills made me naively step forth to buy twelve turkeys for dinner. I envisioned going to a butcher shop and ordering plump, fully cleaned birds wrapped in butcher paper. No one on the food committee told me this was a major task.

Two weeks before the dinner, Lillian, a dinner committee member, and I called a taxi to visit a recommended butcher shop and, if necessary, a poultry farm near the pyramids. The taxi driver was a bit hesitant when we told him where we were going. He pointed out how clean and new his little blue Fiat was. We agreed it looked very nice.

The butcher shop was in a Coptic neighborhood not far from the pyramids. The butcher wiped his bloody hands on his apron and greeted us at the door.

"*Saeeda! Saeeda!* Welcome, *Amrikani!* Turkeys good price. 75 *piastres* a kilo."

The price was double the budget I was given. I emphasized that we would buy *etnasher deek rumi,* twelve turkeys, not just one or two, but it was useless. He wasn't willing to bargain, which was very unusual. Lillian and I gave up and decided to explore the second option, the turkey farm. Our taxi driver raised his eyebrows and shook his head when we gave him the directions.

"*La-a!* No turkeys in taxi," he said.

Of course not. We were going to cook the birds, not raise them, I thought.

As we drove into the turkey farmyard, we were besieged by an off-key chorus of gobblers packed into a pen the size of our entire apartment. After a grinning welcome, the farmer grabbed a scrawny turkey in his arms to show us how "*helwa auwy,*" very beautiful, it was. Our taxi driver got out and stepped into the conversation. He affirmed what he had tried to tell us before. The farmer only sold live turkeys, and not a feather would touch his clean vehicle.

No, no, in taxi!" he told us firmly. "*Abadan, abadan,*" never, never. "Go home to Ma'adi."

We said goodbye to the turkey farmer and got back into the taxi. We were bird-less and frustrated. I then realized that I should have asked an expert, in this case, Salim, for advice on where I could buy reasonably priced turkeys. He was delighted that I turned to him for wise counsel.

"No problem, Madame. I fix. Salim smart." He tapped his head and grinned.

Salim hastened out the door to bicycle to a special butcher shop. He was able to bargain for the turkeys for a reasonable fifty-six *piastres* per kilo (about sixty-five cents a pound). This was not much of a bargain because he paid for the weight of the turkeys while they were still alive, with their craws crammed with cracked corn. The turkeys were delivered to us in dishpans and shopping baskets early in the morning the day before the dinner. They were minus heads but replete with feathers, innards, and dripping blood. Even though I had belonged to a 4-H club, I was a city girl who had never seen a turkey in this condition.

The individual committee members who were going to cook the turkeys needed to pick them up from us that afternoon. What to do now? Floyd, recalling his former farm background, said it was possible to prepare them quickly if he had help. Unfortunately, it was Friday, so Salim was not there to assist. Floyd called Bill Harrison, our Ford Foundation friend, whom he hoped would not mind tackling a messy job. Floyd and Bill started on the task of plucking and cleaning the birds. They worked from eleven a.m. to five p.m., not counting a huge clean-up of feathers, blood, and scraps of meat and bones. Luckily, our telephone was working, so I called the cooking committee to pick up the ready-to-roast turkeys.

Knowing how much pain and suffering went into the holiday turkeys made our appreciation of the dinner even greater. More than eighty people crowded the CAC cafeteria to enjoy the turkeys and many potluck dishes. Luckily, the oil company Americans had "special privileges," so we got canned cranberry sauce and some baked ham as part of the buffet. These two side dishes brought back memories of American Thanksgiving repasts.

▲ ▲ ▲

Troy's and Missy's birthdays, on December 3 and 9, came about the same time as the turkey crisis but were much more fun. Floyd and our neighbor David took some of the apartment children on the train to a nearby suburb to see a small German/Russian circus with dancing bears and acrobats. We also rented a donkey cart to give all the kids in the apartment house rides around the neighborhood. Both Troy and Missy were treated to Salim's special chocolate cake, decorated with red pomegranate seeds instead of frosting. The biggest treat of all, however, was the arrival—finally—of the three metal trunks, my typewriter, two bicycles, and a tricycle we had shipped from Michigan to the seaport in Alexandria. It had taken almost three months for them to clear customs and be delivered to us.

Sonja and Missy loved the bikes and rejoiced in the winter clothing, books, a small phonograph with records, and a folding Barbie doll house. Troy was delighted with his tricycle, Matchbox cars, and the plastic track he could string around his bedroom. We couldn't wait to plug our 8-track player into a transformer in the dining room so we could finally listen to music from home. Our first choice was songs from *Mary Poppins*. The kids had filled the void left by the lack of music or TV with weekly visits to American movies at the Ma'adi Club, a former British sporting club nationalized by the Egyptians and open to everyone. Every Saturday night, we could walk a few blocks to the gardens of the club, sit on wooden benches at an outdoor theater, and watch old American movies—but only the PG- or G-rated ones. Popcorn was just two *piastres*.

▲ ▲ ▲

After the birthdays, it was time to be creative as Christmas approached. The holiday season here was lengthy. The Orthodox Christian Copts, about ten to fifteen percent of the population, celebrated on January 7, two weeks after our non-orthodox observance, so the few stores that sold Christmas goods kept it on display for more than six weeks. However, the usual trappings of an American

Christmas were absent: no Santa Clauses on street corners, no carols on the radio or TV, and no Christmas trees on sale.

Floyd and I went to the Khan Khalili bazaar for several gifts. I found a touristy camel saddle on carved wooden legs, replete with a camel's head, and a Bedouin headdress for Troy. I also asked a local carpenter to make a set of wooden building blocks. He sawed, sanded, and polished about twenty wonderful blocks. We put up an Advent wreath and several other Christmas decorations that I had packed in our trunks. Salim produced a Christmas tree, a feathery, droopy-branched tree that we strung with lights from the trunk and decorations Sonja and Missy had made. On Christmas Eve, Floyd and I took turns reading Christmas stories aloud from the books we had brought with us. Now three years old, Troy still believed Santa Claus would deliver gifts on Christmas Eve.

After story time, we started walking together about six blocks down Road 19 to the Ma'adi Community Church, a small adobe building with about fifty members from different denominations. The building had been a synagogue many years in the past. It was already dark, and for some unknown reason the streetlights were out, so we had to be careful where we walked on the bumpy dirt road. We heard the clip-clop of a donkey behind us. Moving to the side of the road, we saw a woman cloaked in black, head covered with a scarf. She was mounted on a small donkey led by a man in a gray *galabiya*. As they passed, we could see she was carrying a baby wrapped in the end of her long scarf.

"*Assalamu alaikum,*" the man greeted us. Peace be upon you.

The woman pulled her scarf around her face and snuggled the baby closer to her. We stopped to watch them move slowly down the road, held hands with each other, and continued our Christmas Eve journey. The annual Christmas letter to friends and family, one we had written every year since our marriage, summed up our first months in Cairo. No mention was made of Floyd's near-death experience with cholera. We did not want to alarm our family at home in Colorado.

▲ ▲ ▲

December 25, 1971

Dear friends,

We are well settled and "acculturated," although we are still amazed at the contrasts between old and new that we see everyday. A Cairo cinema company filmed a movie called The Angry Young Swinger (English translation) on our street a few days ago. As the cameras and lights moved in, crowds of people gathered to watch. Barefoot donkey drivers, the goat herd from down the street and her sixteen goats, and all the cooks from our apartment building—dressed in white galabiyas *and turbans—clustered around the mini-skirted film star and the cameramen. It's difficult to believe that this ancient Islamic city is also the capital of the Arab film industry.*

Sonja and Missy are enjoying school at Cairo American College... Troy's favorite occupations are trying to tame the twenty cats that haunt our building and riding his tricycle down the road after the herds of goats.

Floyd is teaching graduate classes in communication at American university and serves as assistant chairman of the Economics-Political Science Department. He is launching a new master's program in mass communication, one of the first of its type in the Middle East.

Connie is taking classes in colloquial Arabic and trying to speak nothing but Arabic to the cook. Since we've decided to resist buying a car, bicycles provide much exercise and a means of shopping at the local bazaars ....

Is salaamu aalekum! *Peace be unto you!*
Love, Floyd, Connie, and family.

▲ ▲ ▲

Our first four months in Cairo passed quickly, bridging the gap from euphoria to reality. I had learned some of the practicalities of everyday living: survival Arabic, cultural habits, familiarity with surroundings, prohibitions of Islam, and a forwardness that belied my only-child shyness. The early honeymoon phase of adaptation had swung into true culture shock. Floyd's bout of cholera made it clear that we were in a developing country with all the tension and anxiety that comes with the inability to communicate, misunderstanding of the system—if there was one—and the loss of familiar cultural clues necessary to function daily. And, yes, anger sometimes emerged. However, I could feel myself growing stronger, more outspoken, and more able to deal with whatever came next. And, most importantly, I still saw the physical beauty of Egypt and the humor and friendliness of the people.

Could I put these new-found skills to use to make 1972 a fulfilling year for all of us? Writing had always been a coping mechanism for me, so that became my New Year's resolution. Hopefully, this could extend my near-sighted focus on getting through the day-to-day concerns to the broader context of understanding the people and their social and political issues, and most importantly, the dangers of an impending war with Israel.

▲ ▲ ▲

January 7, 1972

Dear Mama and Daddy,

*It hardly seems like winter here as I sit on the balcony in the sunshine
(about seventy degrees) looking down at the poinsettia trees and
the Sudanese boys next door, who are playing soccer in the street.
In accompaniment to my typing is the call from the mosque for*

afternoon prayers and the sound of the horn man playing tunes on his reed flutes as he proceeds down Road 15 followed by a pied piper bunch of children. The frequent whir of army helicopters intrudes this musical melee.

Our New Year's weekend was spent in Alexandria, a pleasant change from the crowds, traffic, and smog of Cairo. During this off-tourist season, the city is uncrowded, with very few taxis but many horse-drawn hansoms, nice clean air, and the lovely blue Mediterranean Sea. We took a train to Alex (what everyone calls this city) in second-class seats, but it was quite nice and a perfect way to see the bounty of farms along the Nile. We stayed at Schutz School, an American boarding school, where rates were cheap, the food was excellent, and the staff was friendly and interesting. It was a holiday for the students, so very few were in the student residence. Also, the population has diminished from an enrollment of two hundred and fifty before the 1967 War to about seventy students now.

It was mainly a children's holiday: hunting for shells on the beach, walking barefoot on the sand, riding the double-decker trams, and playing on all the climbing equipment in the Schutz schoolyard. Our only touristy event was visiting Montazah Palace and Gardens, King Farouk's last residence, built in 1932, built using an ornate mix of Ottoman and Florentine styles. Again, the contrasts in Egypt are always striking: a new Yugoslavian train traveling beside farms where fellahin *raise irrigation water with an Archimedes screw or an oxen team and water wheel.*

If only we had a better camera and no prohibitions about taking photos. Our Instamatic camera is limited, and we didn't purchase film in the United States. It's expensive here, and processing runs about $1.10 a print, so we have not had any of it developed. Guess we'll save the films up for summer or send them back to you in the States with someone going over soon. Not only is it difficult to take photos here because of the war situation but also because the common Egyptian, also the most photogenic, feels that the camera *robs them of their personhood when a photo is taken. This certainly isn't true of Salim, our cook. He wants to sneak into any photo we take. When we gave him a print of one of the photos sitting on the balcony with Troy on his lap and Sonja and Missy on each side, he took it home to show to his five children and wife.*

Floyd is really enjoying his students. There's such a variety in his classes: no Americans but mostly Egyptians involved in newspapers, radio television, or some form of communication. A nice friendship has grown between Floyd and Tola, a young Russian who's with the United Nations here. He's intelligent, speaks four languages fluently, loves American music and movies, and can speak critically about his country along with pride in it.

We went to a fascinating party the day after Christmas at Tola's apartment. The other guests were all Russian, except for a German professor at the Goethe Institute. None of the women spoke English. Tola's wife communicated with smiles and some German. We had a delicious meal: twelve different salads, pickles, beets, a roast turkey, and dressing, etc. We enjoyed Russian pancakes filled with meat and a six-layer cake for dessert. The Russians proposed at least twenty toasts during the evening, some of them a bit hilarious to us.

"Let's drink to all the children of our children's children."

The conversation was most intriguing. Several old-generation Russians (non-military) but all working on development programs through the UN, tried to impress us with the glories of the Russian countryside, literature, revolution, etc. Tola spent most of the evening arguing with the older Russians about how the younger generation felt. I can't help thinking that we could never have such an evening becoming acquainted with people like this anywhere but here. We came away quite impressed with the fact that the men, including Floyd, all had a common goal: helping an almost hopelessly laggard country get on its feet and develop.

Well, amen, enough for now.
Love, Connie and family

▲ ▲ ▲

Floyd was not in his office on January 26. If he had been, he would have seen and heard thousands of protesters in Tahrir Square. This demonstration was rooted in widespread discontent among the people about various socio-economic issues and political grievances. In response to these protests, President Sadat addressed the nation shortly after the protests began and emphasized his commitment to addressing the issues. However, he also quickly moved to suppress further unrest through police action and arrests of student leaders. This didn't happen just for one day in Tahrir Square; students across the entire country demonstrated and held sit-ins for the whole month. Students in the Tahrir event reported that fifteen hundred people had been arrested, but official sources put the total nearer to one thousand. The protest was forcefully dispersed at five a.m. the next day.

Several of Floyd's students were professionally involved in reporting on the protest for radio and print media. In the following weeks, eight or nine students would gather after class in Floyd's office. With their Turkish coffees in hand, they sat in a close circle to discuss politics and student issues. These discussions were vital to Floyd's understanding of the problems facing the country. They talked about inflation, unemployment, and a general decline in living standards that developed in the aftermath of the 1967 Six-Day War with Israel. Egypt was still reeling from military defeat and loss of territory.

Students and young people felt particularly affected, as they faced limited job opportunities upon graduation. President Nasser had promised free university education and jobs after graduation, but there were not enough jobs for the many graduates. Several of the communication students had enrolled in graduate school because they couldn't find jobs two years after they had received their under-grad diplomas. The defeat in the Six-Day War had severely impacted their pride in Egypt. In the relative safety of Floyd's office, they felt free to criticize the government for not being adequately prepared for the war and for damaging Egypt's standing in the Arab world. They wanted to be more engaged in the political process and to put an end to corruption.

▲ ▲ ▲

After signing the contract with AUC, Floyd had studied the complicated history of the conflict between Egypt and Israel. I relied on him to fill me in as much as possible because I was inundated with hurried preparations to leave our Michigan house. I had readily accepted what we were told about life in Cairo, but not much was said about the possibility that we could be impacted by war. In our home interview, the AUC representative reassured us we would be under the guidance and protection of both the university and the US Embassy in Cairo, which had maintained diplomatic relations with Egypt since the late nineteenth century. He was from California and said his family felt safer in Egypt after the '67 War than in California. Then, too, I knew a war with Israel would be fought on the disputed land, the Sinai Peninsula, 170 miles from Cairo. I hoped that all this reassurance would prove to be true if and when Egypt engaged directly in a war.

However, as winter was almost at an end, the prospect of war was a topic of every conversation in the expatriate community and among the university students. War with Israel seemed to be a necessity for President Sadat. He was making efforts toward a peace that could happen after an Egyptian victory. He had recently expelled Soviet advisers from Egypt and opened diplomatic channels with Washington, DC, which could serve as a crucial mediator in future peace talks. This expulsion of Russians related to the dam and military development was part of Sadat's efforts to reorient the country toward the West marking a shift away from close ties with the Soviet Union.

The prospect of war was becoming more real to us. At home in Ma'adi, blackouts were among the most evident signs of planning for war. Army vehicles had their headlights painted dark blue, and drivers of private cars were asked to turn off their headlights after dusk. This made driving at night dangerous in our quiet, dark suburb. Although it would have been more convenient, I was happy that we did not have a car.

There were other signs of the war effort. As members of the American community who lived on the local economy, we suffered from the same shortages as Egyptians. Rice and coffee were both at a premium and in short supply. Worst of all for us, toilet paper was disappearing from the stores. It was being sent to soldiers getting ready for battle. In place of the thin, stiff Egyptian toilet paper, we had the option of raw cotton or just plain washing with a cloth, soap, and water.

More and more sandbags appeared in front of government buildings and in other strategic locations. We were shocked when we took the kids to the Egyptian Museum, one of our favorite places. The mummy room was fascinating for the kids and the first room we usually visited. When the taxi dropped us off at the door, we were surprised by the walls of sandbags surrounding the perimeter of the building. It was disappointing to find even more sandbags piled around the glass cases, obstructing our view of the artifacts.

Because of Floyd's connections to the Egyptian media, we received many invitations from his students to visit their apartments and homes for meals and conversation. The usual protocol was for the host to close all the drapes, lock the door, and encourage us to sit close together to easily hear each other. One of our hosts was a former journalist for *Al-Ahram,* the leading Arabic newspaper. He had spent three years in prison for his controversial writing about the '67 war. Crackdowns on dissent were common and, because of the impending war, becoming more prevalent.

Foreign journalists and photographers were also targeted. Floyd's colleague, Kennet Love, was arrested for suspected photography of a military convoy. Kennet was a former *New York Times* correspondent in Cairo who covered the Suez Canal crisis in 1956. He was now a correspondent with ABC News and a part-time professor of journalism in Floyd's department. After being interrogated and held for two days, he managed to talk his way out of the situation by invoking his connection to the head of the Egyptian secret service—or so the rumor goes. This whole photography episode prompted us to put away our little Kodak camera.

▲ ▲ ▲

In Cairo, one is always able to find humor in any situation. On a drive with Dale Compton, minister of the Ma'adi Community Church, to visit one of the ancient monasteries outside the city, we passed an area of high fences and what appeared to be a gun turret on a hill. A large sign had a warning in Arabic. As was typical, and much appreciated by us foreigners, it was also translated into English. It read: "SECRET MILITARY BASE."

▲ ▲ ▲

Because we were Americans, with the US supporting Israel, we were under scrutiny. Our telephone conversations were monitored and frequently tape-recorded. I remember picking up the apartment phone to call a taxi for our once-a-week trip to ballet lessons. I started to give directions to the taxi driver when I heard the garbled rewinding of a tape recorder. A few minutes later, I was able to talk without the background noise. In the past, we had engaged a variety of taxi drivers, but recently, the same one, Saeed, was assigned to us. Saeed spoke excellent English and told us he had been in the Air

Force previously and was a captain. I asked him why he was driving a taxi now.

He replied, "I needed a break from the military."

From that day on, he was called Saeed the Spy by all of us.

Taxi Ride

My fortress is a black Mercedes
a taxi with plastic-covered seats.
"Etfel izaz,"roll up the windows
Now latch the door, unroll last week's Time.

I'm incubated, saran-wrapped,
a foreign flower in a see-through box.

Tap, tap, tap, the sound of flesh on glass
Ignore it, read my magazine.
That red light has to change sometime.
I'll just refuse to turn and look.

The driver meets my eyes in the rear-view mirror,
belches a laugh that dares me to look outside.
My sideways glance finds a grin, all cleft from nose
to chin like a shattered watermelon fruit.

Brown eyes askew, the boy's small hand
reaches out to ask for some baksheesh..

The driver laughs again, moves the taxi ahead
while the boy grunts and runs beside the car.
"Unh, unh," he smiles his jack-o-lantern grin.
My wound is opened once again, I hurt

I bleed and cringe with helplessness
against the plastic-covered seat.

6

Death and Dust Storms

Dear Connie,

Grampa died on Monday night from a heart attack. He must have known it was coming because he locked himself in his bedroom. Grandma couldn't get the door open in the morning, so she called her next-door neighbor to help ...

You should have been here. Why are you so far away when you're needed? I'm feeling really sick but will have to plan a funeral now. You're the only grandchild, and he had no other relatives ...

▲ ▲ ▲

The letter from my mother was dated February 16. Floyd had brought it home to me from the university mail room last night: March 10.

I scooted closer to the taxi window to hide my tears from the kids, folded the letter up, and tucked it into my purse, feeling more than a world away from my Colorado family. If only I could have comforted my mother with a hug—even though she didn't like hugs—or at least talked to her by phone. It would have shown her I cared, and it would have assuaged some of my guilt for not having been there. Unfortunately, a quick trip home was out of the question because of the cost and the chance that I might not be allowed back if war broke out. Long-distance calls were not possible, both technically and politically, due to the US's support of Israel.

I last saw my grandfather, Hans (Jim) Grondahl, a few weeks before we left for Cairo. He was eighty-four then. All five of us visited him. He was in his rocking chair in front of the TV in the living room of their small white-frame house in Longmont, Colorado. Although he was short of breath, he asked all kinds of questions about our pending Egyptian adventure. He recalled his own excitement about leaving Denmark when he was in his early twenties to start a new life in the United States, settling in Lyle, Minnesota. He joined a Danish friend there and set up a small farm, married my Norwegian grandmother, Bettie Lundblad, and had a daughter, Mildred Pauline, my mother. When Bettie contracted TB, the family moved to Brush, Colorado, to be near the Swedish TB sanatorium, where Bettie recovered in the sunny, dry Colorado climate. After her recovery, they relocated to Longmont, where he was employed at the Longmont Creamery. He recalled his adventurous spirit as an immigrant. When we said goodbye, Grampa wished us well on an adventure he would have loved.

All I could do now was write to my mother, trying to console her and telling her how sorry I was for not being with her at such a difficult time. I asked Floyd to find someone to take the letter to the States to be mailed. One of the deans took it on his trip to the university's New York office. My mom never mentioned the letter later, and it was not in the group she saved in the notebook she gave me.

Troy and Missy went along on our weekly trip to Sonja's ballet lesson because they wanted to browse the upscale shops in Zamalek and stop at Luigi's Italian Ice Cream Store after the lesson. Zamalek was a fancy neighborhood on Gezira, an island in the Nile, where political leaders, artists, and public figures lived. It was also the site of the Gezira Club, a British-established sporting club.

The taxi made a quick halt at the steps of the two-story building that housed Madame Laurella's ballet studio. We seated ourselves in our usual places just outside the door to a large open room with a long ballet barre on one side. We could hear Madame Laurella's demanding commands in French set to piano accompaniment played by an elderly Turkish lady. The seven pre-teen girls rehearsed for yet another performance.

Russian ballet training in a Muslim country? Hard to fathom. But, like film, theater, and opera, it was part of the culture. It was fascinating to see strong Islamic traditions and practices in the personal and public lives of Egyptians coexisting with ballet, opera, plays, and sexy movies produced by the "Hollywood of the Arab World."

The Cairo Ballet Company had its beginnings in the 1960s with support from Soviet scholarships for Egyptian dancers to study at famous institutions like the Bolshoi in Russia. Madame Laurella had retired from the Ballet Company to open her own studio. Madame Laurella's eighty-year-old mother greeted us and sat down to chat. We had a trilingual conversation: a little French, some Arabic, and a bit of English. In the meantime, Missy kept Troy busy with the matchbox cars he had brought with him. The hour passed slowly, and we were ready to have our ice cream and do some window shopping. When we came out of the building, the wind was stirring up clouds of dust and trash from the street. I was worried about the four-block walk to the shopping area. I told the kids it would be better to get a taxi to go back to Ma'adi. Troy was complaining about missing an ice cream treat when an old Mercedes taxi pulled over and offered us a ride. We settled together in the roomy but smelly back seat of the cab.

Within ten minutes, sand-colored dust was whirling around the taxi windows and seeping through the cracks into our noses and mouths. This was like a blizzard at home in Colorado. It was the *khamseen* or *haboob,* fifty days of strong dust storms that lift and carry large amounts of sand and dust from the ground into the atmosphere. Evidently, these storms can create walls of dust several kilometers high and wide. If there had been such an innovation as a weather report in English, we would have been warned of the intensity of this sandstorm and skipped our weekly ballet lesson.

I told the taxi driver to take us to Maʿadi, the oft-repeated Road 19, Number 48, but as far as I could tell through the obscured windows, we were headed in the opposite direction toward old Cairo. As we came to the City of the Dead, a wall of dust limited our visibility to about twenty feet. This huge centuries-old cemetery and mausoleum area honored the dead and housed the living. Just a few of the thousands of homeless people who sheltered there were visible through the swirling sand. Cairo was swamped with over-population and a severe housing shortage. Many individuals resorted to squatting within mausoleums and tomb enclosures, turning them into improvised housing in which entire families lived. The heavy yellowish-gray dust gave the place an even eerier feeling.

Two of the taxi windows would not close completely, so the gritty dust was making all of us cough. The contact lenses I wore felt like two huge boulders, but I couldn't see past my nose without them and found glasses inadequate. I hadn't even thought about the dry, dusty climate I was entering. Dumb? Yes.

"*Min fadlik, hena mish kuwayʾyes. Ihna awzin Maʿadi,*" I said, using the best Arabic I could muster in a polite request to not stop here but to take us to Maʿadi. The driver laughed, pulled over on a side street, and got out to wipe the windows with a rag. When he got back in, I repeated my request without the "please" to get us to Maʿadi and the safety of our apartment.

"*Madame, Maʿadi hena,*" He laughed again.

"*La-a! Maʿadi mish hena!*" I leaned forward and enunciated. "This is not Maʿadi."

"*Maʿalesh,*" he responded.

"What are we going to do, Mommy?" Missy asked.

"We're not getting out of the car; that's for sure," Sonja said.

Troy huddled closer under my arm. "I just want to go home!"

The driver told me to wait for a little while, but I was beginning to panic. What was he planning to do? Drop us off in a cemetery teeming with poverty-stricken people in the middle of a sandstorm? Or worse? I pointed at the broken taxi meter.

"*Yemken itneen geneh?*"

I was hopeful that offering to pay him two pounds would be persuasive.

"*Madame, Ma'adi talata geneh.*"

I scooted back on the seat, looked at the kids, and shook my head.

"*Tayyib.*" Okay. I agreed to three pounds.

My panic subsided when I realized the wisdom of waiting for a break in the storm, but I had already offered him an exorbitant sum. Although it was only equivalent to about six American dollars, we were not rich tourists. After twenty long minutes of waiting until the wind died down, we pulled out of the City of the Dead and slowly drove through the blowing sand and dust to Ma'adi. We arrived exhausted but safe and sound. What's the old saying "penny-wise and three pounds foolish"?

We shared our scary sandstorm experience with Floyd before dinner. I needed more than retelling the story. I wanted a way to release tension and recoup my composure. Our only newspaper was *The Egyptian Gazette,* a poor-quality weekly English language newspaper, in contrast to *Al Ahram,* the best Arabic newspaper in the Middle East. I saved all the *Gazettes* in a basket with a few old *Time* and *Newsweek* magazines from the Hilton Hotel. I pulled out the newspapers.

"Let's have a snowball fight," I suggested.

Floyd thought I was delusional. The kids were suspicious.

I tore newspaper pages up, wadded them into balls, and started throwing them at Floyd and the kids. We all dived in, wadded up the balls, hid behind dining room chairs, and hurled our stress at each other. Salim hurried in from the kitchen to see what was wrong. I threw a "snowball" at him. He finally caught on and joined us by challenging Troy to a contest. Laughter and fun! And then we finally sat down at the dining table while Salim cleaned up the weeks of Gazette snowballs.

▲ ▲ ▲

Sandstorm season also signaled the beginning of spring in Egypt.

▲ ▲ ▲

March 20, 1972

Dear Mama and Daddy,

As I typed the date, it occurred to me that today is the first day of spring. There doesn't seem to be much change in seasons from winter to spring here, except that orange blossoms, bougainvillea, and some other unknown blooms are welcoming the season. We've had a taste of the khamsin, a possible fifty days of dusty and windy weather. Egyptians celebrate a special spring holiday called Sham El-Nessim, which has roots going back to ancient Egyptian traditions. The name means "smelling the breeze." Special smoked fish, boiled eggs, and thick balady bread are part of the celebration.

We got your pretty Easter cards and egg decorations last week. We decorated our apartment door with the cards and some other seasonal drawings. The result of this is that the other little kids in the building, about fifteen of them, came knocking at our door.

"Mrs. Shoemaker, would you draw me a bunny like the one on your door?"

The poor holiday-starved American kids!

I found out today that Easter will be remembered here after all. The Coptic Church celebrates Easter, of course, and eggs in all colors are a major part of their holiday. The Copts fast for forty days before Easter, eliminating meat and various staples from their diets. Then, on Easter day, red-colored eggs are part of a fun ritual. Groppi's, a large candy and pastry shop leftover from the British occupation, has chocolate bunnies and eggs.

Our church had a difficult time trying to decide when to celebrate Easter. It seems we have a choice between Western Easter on the second of April and Eastern (Coptic) Easter on the ninth. We chose the ninth because CAC gives a four-day holiday that weekend. We're planning a sunrise service in one of the lovely gardens in Maadi, at the home of the Harrisons, where Troy has his nursery school. We'll have the service at six-thirty a.m. and then a breakfast of juice, rolls, sausage, and coffee. The teenagers in the church are planning an Easter egg hunt at CAC later in the morning, so the kids will have a ball hunting eggs among the cactus and flower beds around the school.

We're hoping to move to a villa soon because we're quite crowded here in the apartment. The rooms are nice but small, and we miss having a yard and garden. The villas owned by the university are all lovely and not much more expensive than the apartments, since the university subsidizes them too. Two families are leaving in June. One, a Chinese professor of chemistry, was in severe culture shock, and the other one was fired, so maybe we'll be placed into one or the other of these villas. AUC was kind enough to allow these families to stay in the villas until they had found jobs elsewhere.

Much love,
Connie

▲ ▲ ▲

Floyd's mass communications program was developing well with high demand for the classes among local media professionals with a few international students mixed in with the group. He was working hard on curriculum development for new classes, expanding the library's collection of communication and journalism books, and creating standards for the master's degree program that, hopefully, would make it the best one in the Middle East. The definitive textbook he contributed to, *Diffusion of Innovations* with Dr. Everett Rogers, was being widely distributed in Cairo. Unfortunately, there were no copyright laws in Egypt, so copies were cheaply mimeographed and sold locally. As Floyd always did, he was putting all his brain power and energy into the challenge of establishing a new program. He needed to focus only on this task and not be bothered by any other hurdles the culture presented.

His students had fun teaching him about Egyptian culture. Students from his Communication of Innovations class invited him to lunch in the Mousky bazaar. They suggested he order *kushari*, which is Egypt's national comfort dish and a widely popular street food. It mixes pasta, Egyptian fried rice, vermicelli, and brown lentils and is topped with chickpeas, a garlicky tomato sauce, garlic vinegar, and crispy fried onions. Decorating the top is a round white object with a sprinkle of red sauce in the middle. The students told him it was a lamb's eyeball, an Egyptian delicacy that should be swallowed whole. Knowing that he needed to display the innovative qualities he was teaching, they decided he could not refuse to try something new. He promptly took the "eyeball" with a spoon and swallowed it. It tasted just like a boiled egg. And it was!

Floyd was gaining professional recognition in nearby Lebanon. He was invited to be a panelist at an international communications conference at the American University in Beirut, where he would also meet Steve, the brother of Peter Garrett, Floyd's best friend in high school. Steve was finishing two semesters of teaching at AUB and was accompanied by his wife, Marta.

▲ ▲ ▲

April 24, 1972

Hooray! Floyd gets out of here for a breather next Monday. The university is paying his way to Beirut to an international conference on communications in the Middle East. He'll take part as a panel participant since he didn't have time to prepare a paper. It will be a good chance to meet people and talk about jobs next year. He'll probably be gone for a week and will shop for our needs in Beirut, although US products are sky-high there.

So many university people here are getting ready for paid home leave of four to six weeks, but two-year hires like us only get vacation time and no paid travel time. We will just have to wait. It's hard to believe, but in June we'll be only a year away from our departure date. Life here has been a good experience for all of us, but this time of year makes everyone ready for an "escape" to somewhere else ...

▲ ▲ ▲

Even though our contract with AUC didn't end until June of 1973, we had to plan for our return to the States and, hopefully, to Colorado. We had no idea if Floyd could find a job from Cairo without going to the States for an interview. Floyd's university salary was paid both in Egyptian pounds for our daily necessities and in American dollars deposited directly into our US bank account. Egyptian income tax was extremely high, about thirty percent with a war tax added on. Everything was taxed, including our housing allowance, so not much was left for other expenditures. American dollars could be used for airfare if required, but we were still paying the mortgage and property tax on our Michigan house. We hoped to save some of the dollars for resettling in the States.

▲ ▲ ▲

May 31, 1972

I discovered we were spending more money on food than most
families of our size. I can't put my finger on anything exactly but
think Salim has been cheating us. I keep daily accounts, but it's very
difficult to check on prices. Anyway, rather than firing him, we've
given him the chance to keep our food down to LE fifteen per week;
that's about thirty-five American dollars. Food here is inexpensive,
at least all fresh food is very cheap, so we should have been living
within our salary, which we haven't been. It's taken as a matter of
course that the cooks add a bit to the food bill, just a national trait,
but we evidently have let him slip by and add more than a bit.
We pay him LE twenty-one, which is more than most college grads
make but typical for cooks and suffragis. He has five children,
so I imagine that's where the money has gone. I'm beginning to
learn how to handle servants. Firmly!

▲ ▲ ▲

A more immediate concern was our upcoming summer vacation. Where could we travel within our budget? We considered the island of Cyprus as an August vacation spot. Cyprus Airways had a special for a party of six, so we planned to go with Dale Compton, the minister at our church, and his family and possibly stay in an American mission house there. Hopefully, the Greek food on the island would help to fatten Floyd up after his twenty-pound weight loss a few months ago. We borrowed a scale from a neighbor to weigh each of us. Troy, now three, had gained more than three pounds since our last weigh-in in November, and Sonja and Missy each weighed a bit more. Fortunately, I had lost a few pounds from all my bike riding and not snacking all the time as I did in the States. Sonja, almost eleven, was getting quite tall compared to Missy, nine and a half, who still looked like a little girl. Our apartment cat, Hatshepsut (Patches) was the fattest cat in the building.

Our social life exploded that spring. Going away parties happened every weekend as company people were transferred out of Cairo to other destinations. Missy and Sonja felt sad because new friends planned to leave Cairo for other postings. We said goodbye to one of Missy's best friends, Nadine, by inviting her on a farewell ride on a felucca boat. Salim prepared a picnic lunch of potato chips and fried chicken, so we could have an American menu. Of course, Sonja and Troy joined us. Sonja had made friends but was hesitant to become too close to them. She was the most affected by our many moves in the States for Floyd's education. She didn't want to suffer the loss of friends again.

Sonja began reading when she was two years old. Books were her friends, her teachers, and her comfort zone. She was the CAC library's best customer. Sandra Gamal, the librarian, would chat with her about each book when she returned it. On our taxi trips, Sonja would open her bag, pull out the current book, and begin reading. It was a way to avoid the taps on the window by handicapped beggars. She continued to show talent for ballet, and although she was shy, she endured the demanding French spoken by Madame Laurella and the occasional corrective tweak of Madame's baton. In a May recital at the Italian Cultural Center, she was chosen to do two solos. We made an event of the recital since this was the first time Floyd had seen Sonja dance in Cairo. Our apartment neighbors went to the program with their small daughters, who adored ballet. We all celebrated Sonja's performance by having ice cream at the Sheraton Hotel. I applauded Sonja's skills and her growing confidence.

Even the most far-out recreational activity in Ma'adi was celebrated in the spring. We joined the Square Dance Club for their final event. The caller was an oil company engineer who had organized square dance groups in Kuwait, Iran, and other places they had lived. The group included two Egyptian men married to American CAC teachers. The men seemed to have two left feet and an innate fear of touching a woman's hand. Floyd and I got into quite a few muddles and made many mistakes but laughed a lot.

Spring semester finals at the university were finished and grades submitted, so it was time to party on campus too. In addition to several other couples, we were invited to the university president's house. Dr. Byrd was the acting AUC president, replacing Dr. Christopher Thoron, whose illness had forced him to withdraw after three years. He and his lovely Filipina wife lived in a penthouse apartment overlooking the Nile with cats, birds, a baby, and several servants.

Floyd's students eagerly entertained him, too. One of the most memorable invitations was to the perfume factory owned by Ameena and her husband. Their three-story villa was situated near a large concrete building that housed a room of large containers of resins, spices, and essential oils, like rose and jasmine. Other rooms housed copper vats that distilled the oils and mixing areas that contained blending tanks where workers mixed essential oils to create fragrance bases. No alcohol bases were permitted because of Islamic restrictions. By the time we reached the bottling area, our heads spun, and we were literally dizzy from the bombardment of fragrances.

▲ ▲ ▲

Reviewing Sonja and Missy's first year at CAC filled us with appreciation for the high quality of education it offered. The girls had been exposed to Egyptian history with weekly field trips this spring. Missy's third-grade curriculum included a unit on ancient Egyptian art, transportation, and agriculture. Her teacher, an American married to an Egyptian, had organized weekly tours of museums that focused on these objectives. An annual Egyptian projects day showcased Egyptian dances the students had learned, ceremonies, and models of Egyptian villages. More than four hundred people came to see the Egypt Festival.

An operetta, a shortened version of *Hansel and Gretel,* was also a feature of the year. Missy was a cookie child, very appropriate for her sweet tooth. All the students at CAC learned to play the fluto-phone. In fifth grade, they could choose an instrument to play. Sonja had switched from her first choice, the cornet, to the more musical clarinet and performed in a program with the school band. The instruments had to be returned to the school for the summer, so if she wanted to practice during vacation, we would need to get an instrument from the States or hunt for a clarinet in hopes that one of the expat families had one.

My teaching life had expanded this year with tutoring English to a Japanese Embassy eight-year-old so he could enter CAC in the fall and teaching technical English to a class of Egyptian geologists at the Gulf of Suez Petroleum Company. They needed to improve their communication skills as they interfaced with their American counterparts. I also accepted the job of teaching a CAC journalism class of politically-minded Yugoslavians who wanted to put their radical views into the student newspaper. In contrast to this was substituting in the nursery school some of us had created last fall for English-speaking two- to four-year-olds in Maadi. Twice a week, Troy and seven other kids played games, painted, sang, and drove the volunteer teachers crazy from nine a.m. to noon at various villas in the neighborhood.

Our first academic year in Cairo was filled with trials, adventures, and adjustments. We had emerged whole and ready for another year.

A Last Goodnight

His fingers numb, he fumbled for the hook
to latch the bedroom door behind him.
"There now, she can't come in to pry
when I don't answer in the morning,"
the thought competing with his thudding pulse.
Across the miles of kitchen lay her door
ajar a foot to catch the cook-stove warmth.
"I should have said goodnight," she thought
while winding tight the noisy brass alarm.
"He looked too pale, too white."

The ritual of sixty years gave strength to
hands, which seemed to float in front of him.
The scarecrow shirt and trousers hanging slack
on muscles lax since farming days
each button challenging his feinting thoughts.

They had been close once. He was twenty-two,
and she was flattered by the husky Dane
who had moved into her Minnesota town.
Farm chores and hopes and sharing the same bed
had made life warm and full in those first days.

The break between them—when did it begin?
After their only child was born? When she
refused to sleep in the same room with him?
Or was it when he sold the farm and moved
six hundred miles to cure her lung disease?

She placed the purple marker in the Book.
"It's the way he lives—cigars and beer
and bickering. He's always bickering.
That's why he had the heart attack.
And yet, he seemed so all alone tonight.

He left his slippers on because he knew
if he bent down the pain would tear his chest.
Shunning the comfort of the light, he pulled
the metal chain and sat, then propped himself
up on the pillows, plucking close the quilt.

"It's all just part of the routine," he thought,
"The latch, the clothes, the light, the bed,
and death.
She'll hear and think I'm all right, or does she even care?
No, not enough to say a last goodnight."

7

Summer Sun and Darkness

FLOYD RETURNED FROM Beirut excited and positively glowing about his experience at the National East-West Communications conference held in the mountains at Beit Meri. Just getting away from Cairo did him good. He described Beirut as beautiful: clean sea water, forests of cedars, and green mountains. He had enjoyed his visit with Steve and Marta.

▲ ▲ ▲

June 10, 1973

The Garretts were marvelous to Floyd and did all the shopping we had listed because Floyd's meeting wasn't in the city. Marta took the list of things (ballet-toe shoes, powdered milk, earplugs, etc.) and shopped for several days to find what we needed. Then she packed up an old suitcase of theirs with toys from her children (they're moving to California in a week and were discarding them), candy, and all the items. We felt like it was Christmas in May when Floyd arrived. I never thought the kids would be delighted with powdered milk, but they were pleased with a huge can of the French powdered kind that tasted quite good after the boiled cow's milk, which we use primarily in cocoa ... Pasteurized milk is almost impossible to find. I was pleased with a big jar of Nescafe, which has been taken off the market here, as have most imports. You can still get a few of these things but at ridiculous prices. Troy got a selection of little Matchbox cars and some plastic construction blocks. Sonja received a pair of

91

*pink silk-toe shoes for just twenty Lebanese pounds, six dollars in
American money, and Missy got some of her favorite candy ...*

*As you may have read in your newspapers, the staff of the
American Interests Section of the Embassy here has been cut in
half and is being posted to other cities. None of them are eager to go
since they're settled and have jobs to do here, but half of the staff
of twenty will have to leave. We're acquainted with quite a few
embassy people. The former American ambassador was well-
received, but his replacement has never been officially recognized
by the Egyptian government. This inaction seems to be part of
the antagonism toward the US support of enemy Israel. Floyd's
conference in Beirut dealt with the Middle East crisis and improved
communication between East and West. Much discussion was spent
on the bias of news reporting respecting Palestinian and the Israeli
situation. Newsmen and editors from all over the world attended ...*

▲ ▲ ▲

After hearing about Beirut, called the Paris of the Middle East, Sonja
and Missy voted for a trip there so they could see department stores,
supermarkets, and even McDonald's-type fast food places. Missy
especially craved American hamburgers again. Another chance for
shopping came from the annual swap shop that the church held this
spring. What fun after not seeing a sale for almost a year! Much of
the clothing came from London or Paris. We bought Troy a good
winter jacket, short jackets and coats for Sonja and Missy, and three
lovely dresses for Sonja. A small phonograph was a great bargain, so
now we could listen to some of the records we brought with us. The
variety of things we do with our time at home since we don't have
television amazes us. Of course, we miss the TV entertainment, but
we put together puzzles, read, listen to music on our 8-track player
hooked up to a transformer, practice piano and clarinet, and go to
Friday movies at the Ma'adi Club.

▲ ▲ ▲

Summer 1972 arrived, and the American population in Ma'adi had diminished. Company employees vacationed or moved on to other sites. The university faculty who had finished their contracts prepared to leave, and the new faculty wouldn't arrive until September. Floyd taught Sunday through Thursday in the summer with Fridays and Saturdays off so that gave us more time than the usual broken up weekend of Friday (Muslim holiday) and Sunday (Christian holiday).

We planned a pleasant summer starting with another ballet recital for Sonja, this time at the large theater in Ewart Hall on the AUC campus. The polished production was well worth the strict instruction from Madame Laurella. A reviewer in *The Egyptian Gazette* mentioned her name three times. It called her solos "elegantly graceful."

We spent two relaxing weekends in Alexandria, Egypt's principal seaport on the western edge of the Nile Delta, about 114 miles northwest of Cairo, where the Nile reaches the Mediterranean Sea. What a lovely cosmopolitan city! Founded by Alexander the Great in 331 BCE, it had long been a center of learning and commerce. It still maintained its reputation as an intellectual center; however, it faced challenges from political repression following Nasser's regime. Despite these challenges, Alexandria continued to host various cultural events, including literary gatherings and theatrical performances that celebrated both Egyptian and international works. The population included Egyptians from various backgrounds along with communities of Greeks and Italians who had historically contributed to the city's cosmopolitan character. However, many expatriates had begun to leave because of the changing political climate and economic uncertainties.

We spent the first weekend at a small villa in Agami, a beach settlement ten kilometers from Alexandria. We shared the villa with our neighbors, the Johns, and spent every day on the beach. The ocean was still, and the sand was white. The only drawback was the oil, which lay in ugly spots on the sand and transferred to our swimsuits, towels, and beach toys. We took a can of benzene along to clean everything.

The next weekend, we went back to Schutz American School in downtown Alexandria, where we had stayed previously. Their Greek cook made good American-style food, which satisfied our appetite for home. We toured King Farouk's palace and grounds for one outing and a downtown movie theater for another. Alex had a clean, Mediterranean atmosphere, fewer people than Cairo, and less dirt and noise.

Floyd and I enjoyed browsing the small antique shops. A friendly Jewish clockmaker encouraged us to visit with him and peruse his array of clocks, watches, and sundials. When the top of the hour arrived, the shop became an orchestra of bass booms, treble half notes, and tinkling chimes. He invited us for a cup of tea and told us about the dwindling Jewish population in the city in which he had been born.

"My grandfather's grandfather's grandfather came to *Iskandariya* from Judea. He wanted a better life for his family. Life changes, but Iskandriya is still my city," he said. He pointed across the street to a synagogue, a school and several other Jewish-owned shops, one of which had a closed sign. As we sipped our tea, we were treated to personal reminiscences of Alexandria when it was the intellectual capital of the Middle East, welcoming to all cultures. I wanted a memory of this shop, its owner, and its place in Egyptian history. Floyd agreed with my suggestion to buy a clock to take home to the US. We decided on a wall-hanging clock with a brass pendulum. It had a subdued tick-tock and a lovely chime to announce the half and whole hours. Most importantly, it had a small silver plaque at the base that read, "J. Rosenbloom, Alexandria."

▲ ▲ ▲

Hooray! The university told us we would have possession of our villa by July 15 after the Chinese chemistry professor and his family move out. The university had canceled his contract, but he had difficulty finding a job, so he was allowed to stay for three additional months. I felt sorry for him and his family; however, we couldn't wait to have more room and a garden. The villa was close to the Ma'adi Club, a source of relaxation and play we had recently discovered. The club, established in 1910, was a relic of the British occupation of Egypt. The Brits wanted a social club where they could engage in sports, leisure activities, and high tea in the garden with, of course, other Britons. When the Brits were kicked out in 1956, the club was nationalized and opened to Egyptians, Americans, Russians, and expats from all countries.

Troy learned to swim in the club's Olympic-sized pool by taking lessons from Ibrahim, a former Olympic swimmer who, fifty years later, had become the swim instructor. I was surprised by Ibrahim's method of instruction when I took Troy early one morning for his first swim lesson. Ibrahim put swim fins on him, attached a small harness around his chest, and told him to jump into the deep water at the end of the pool. There was no shallow water. From the sidelines, Ibrahim demonstrated how Troy should move his arms and kick. I bit my lip as I watched, but Ibrahim was charming and told me not to worry. Initially hesitant, Troy was persuaded into the pool and was thrilled to discover he could float.

"Look, Mom, I can swim!" he shouted as he splashed the water with his arms.

The lessons continued every Saturday until Troy could be released from the harness and take off on his own. Missy enjoyed English riding lessons at the club on her favorite horse, Mabruk, one of the stable of horses provided. The club had every activity possible: horseshoes, lawn bowling, tennis, a stable of horses, a huge sand pile for little kids (forbidden to Troy because of the tarantula Sonja saw there), tea or light lunch in the well-designed gardens, and our most beloved activity, old American and British movies at the Ma'adi theater, replete with popcorn. Our favorites were *To Kill a Mockingbird*, *Planet of the Apes,* and *The Sound of Music.* So far, American movies had not been banned like all other American products.

It's amazing to see how quickly one's perspective can change from minor, everyday inconveniences to actual life-and-death concerns. One of those summer Mondays started with the need to confront Salim about the food that was disappearing from the refrigerator. I told him I had planned to use the large bowl of leftover spaghetti and meatballs for supper on Sunday but couldn't find them or the stuffed squash in the refrigerator.

"Ah, Madame, Salim sorry. Food not good. I put in *zibala. Ma'alesh.*"

I reminded him that we were spending a lot of money on food, so to ask me next time before he threw away anything good. He continued with his "Salim sorrys" while I hurried to get Troy ready for Monday preschool at the Harrison's house.

The telephone rang with its usual halting tone. When I picked up the receiver and said "Hello," I heard an accented voice shout, "Madame Shoemaker," and then nothing; there was no sound until I heard the whir of a tape recorder rewinding. Typical inept spying, I thought, and banged the receiver down. Just as I was helping Troy to tie his sneakers, it rang again. This time I just ignored it.

When we went downstairs to get my bike, we couldn't find it in the usual row of bicycles under the apartment carport. Where was it? We walked around the building and found it lying in the grass by the outdoor Turkish toilets used by the cooks and staff. The front tire was flat. I said a few English words that weren't yet in my Arabic vocabulary and wheeled the lame bike to the main door. One of the *suffragis* was having his morning coffee. He saw my problem, examined the tire, and went to get a bicycle pump to fill it with air. After fifteen minutes, Troy and I headed to the Harrison's.

The kids were already busy with a messy finger-painting activity on the patio with the help of Jamila's mom. All the mothers stayed to talk, which was unusual, and were seated in a circle on the covered veranda. Some of them were wiping tears from their eyes. I joined the group.

Anne Marie explained the emotion that enveloped the circle of moms. Three Americans had been killed in an auto accident last night on Road 15. An army truck had hit the small VW filled with five American passengers headed to the Catholic church for a rehearsal of the Ma'adi Players, a recently organized acting group. The headlights of both vehicles had been painted dark blue, as required during the war effort. Tom O'Connor, an American Oil Company (AMOCO) employee, was driving. Seated next to him was his wife, Jeanette. In the middle of the back seat was Jenny Allison, play director and wife of a CBS foreign correspondent. On each side of Jenny, next to the windows, sat an AUC husband and wife from Pittsburgh, unnamed at that point. The impact of the crash threw Jenny Allison out the back and into bushes at the side of the road. Jeanette in the front seat and the AUC couple in the back were killed. They had two children. Other occupants were severely injured.

The reaction to this tragedy ran the gamut among the circle of mothers:

"Those damned, stupid Egyptian soldiers."

"What will those poor children do?"

"Thank God, it didn't happen to our family."

My first reaction, as I write this more than fifty years later, is "What were we thinking when we exposed our three children to all the dangers that came with life in a developing country, especially one preparing for war?"

My second thought is more compassionate. We were young, naive and believed we could play a small part in changing the world. At the time, our sense of purpose for being in Egypt over-ruled fear of the dangers. We trusted the innate goodness of the Egyptian people and the support system of the university, CAC, and our friends and neighbors. We took extra precautions with the kids' activities and confirmed plans that the university had for us during an altercation with Israel. It's true that the accident was a tragedy, but it was unintentional.

Insha Allah, God willing, we would continue to be safe.

Zibala

Not since the Vikings dwelt high in Valhalla
has there been an invention like our cook's
zibala.
It's the usual smelly, tin garbage container,
but it takes the first prize as the "missing explainer."
When the Mister or Madame asks, "Where
did the roast go?"
Then the cook can just say, "Oh, my lady,
you must know,
Praise be to our Allah,
It's in the zibala!"
When the kids storm the icebox, they think
Mother Hubbard
just cleaned out the spider from inside
her cupboard.
Oh, the leftover cakes and the puddings that
vanish
are enough to make us wish forever to
banish
from the kitchen, that cook who grows
fatter and fatter
on the goodies left over from each plate
and each platter.
"Praise be to our Allah,
It's in the zibala!"

8

A Villa, No Less

NUMBER 48, ROAD 19. Our new home.

The university van parked in front of an elegant two-story stucco house with a red-tiled roof. It was set on a huge corner lot surrounded by a well-trimmed hedge and filled with grape vines and a garden of trees: mangoes, papayas, oranges, mandarins, and lemons.

Sonja, Missy, and Troy couldn't wait to get out and explore the home we'd been anticipating for almost ten months. Hatshepsut (Patches) the cat was eager to get out, too. The university had already delivered our belongings, which consisted of the same old luggage and trunks and the few possessions we'd accumulated. The university supplied all the furniture, linens, kitchen appliances, pots and pans, and china. Speaking of kitchens, Salim was already there to welcome us. His new work site was a step up from the apartment, and he proudly welcomed us at the gate, scooping up Troy to give him a hug. Not wanting affection at that moment, Troy struggled to get down and explore the house.

When we walked through the gate, the scent of *yasmin* welcomed us. The arch over the gate was covered with vines of white Jasmine blossoms. I remembered seeing the flowers sold in lacy necklaces to passersby on the street or to taxi passengers at stop signs. It was a sweet welcome to our villa.

No history of the house was provided, but we guessed it was built for a British family sometime during the latter part of the British colonization of Egypt, which was from 1882 to 1922. The Brits built the Ma'adi Sporting Club in the center of this neighborhood.

The house seemed huge although it had only three bedrooms. The front door opened into a foyer, which welcomed us to a huge dining area with a table to seat eight. The ceilings on the first floor were twenty feet in height and had all been freshly painted a flat white. An arch at the rear of this area opened into a small music room, replete with a piano and a desk. One could open a door from this room into a screened veranda that faced the back gardens. The entryway and dining area floors were made of shiny terrazzo, a composite of marble, quartz, and granite—beautiful and made to last forever. A tiny guest bathroom with a sink and toilet was just inside the front door. Sonja peaked at the sink to see a tiny frog staring back at her. Evidently, he had come to visit through the drainpipe.

A quick turn to the right of the front door took us to a long, narrow living room with a parquet floor, featuring two sofas, two chairs, and a fireplace. On the other side of the dining room were two small kitchens, one with a refrigerator and a table topped with metal and the other with a sink, a *butagaz* stove, cupboards, and worktables.

Troy yelled at us from the landing of the two-tiered staircase to the second floor.

"Watch this, Dad!" he said as he proceeded to slide precariously down the lower banister.

That became a "no-no" in the future. Sonja and Missy had a huge bedroom on the second floor with a high ledge under windows set on multiple storage cabinets—a perfect place for Missy's Barbie house and assorted pretend items. We could never determine why there were three single beds, but it was handy for overnight guests and slumber parties. Next to the girls' room was a large master bedroom with a small, white stucco fireplace. Two single beds were placed together on one wall, giving us the double bed we had hoped for. A dusty balcony, overgrown with bougainvillea vines, looked out on the expanse of fruit trees and grass behind the house. Troy had a smaller bedroom next to ours but lots of floor space for his plastic racetrack and collection of Matchbox cars.

The second floor featured both a small shower room and a large, full bathroom with a tub, sink, toilet, and a separate bidet. Heat for the tub, of course, came from a *butagaz* tank that had to be turned on to heat water prior to showering or bathing. The high ceilings, thick walls, and shutters on the windows provided relief from the heat in the summer. There was no real need for air conditioning, although the university provided two fans. In the winter, we discovered that cold permeated the house and our bones. Our only refuge was to bundle up or, when necessary, to huddle around a *butagaz* heater in the dining or living room. It was always difficult to believe that Egypt could be so cold indoors in the winter.

Salim walked us around the outside of the house and introduced us to Ayyoub, the gardener, a smiling, muscular man who was about thirty years old. His *galabiya* was tucked up around his severely bowed legs, and his feet were bare. Although he spoke just a smattering of English, he proudly led us on an expedition through his beloved garden. As if they were his children, he gave us the name of each tree and plant. Near the front porch, he had planted waist-high red clay pots with large ferns. Smaller pots of geraniums lined the path from the front door to the back garden. These pathways of packed soil were perfect "roads" for Troy to race the new Big Wheels he had acquired at the spring rummage sale. This became problematic for Ayyoub's relationship with Troy when a Big Wheel accident occurred and he ran into one of the pots.

Salim finished his tour by showing us a garage at the back of the property.

"House dog sleep here," he said, pointing to an old rug behind a bush at the back of the garage. This excited Troy, but we couldn't find the dog.

We looked inside the garage and saw a sleeping cot and chairs, a convenient place for a servant to stay overnight or just take a break.

The servants' toilet was at the back of the house. It was a typical Turkish squat toilet: a small concrete slab with a hole in the ground and places for feet. A water tap for cleansing was by the hole. This, too, of course, was intriguing for not-quite four-year-old Troy. It occurred to me then that something was missing. There was no washing machine. What do we do to wash clothes for our five family members? The university promised to find a washing machine and send us a *makwagi,* a laundress, to assist. This is how we met Semeha, who became part of our household for the next two and half years.

Semeha was about forty, a heavy-set, big-bosomed woman. Her laugh was as large as her heart. She adored children. Unfortunately, she was not married but told us she was still hopeful about finding a husband. Semeha smiled a lot, always revealing two large protruding upper teeth. In the six weeks it took the university to find a washing machine, Semeha washed our clothes in the bathtub using a washboard to rub out recalcitrant stains, rinsing and then wringing out clothes in her strong, rough hands. She hung them on the clothesline to the side of the house and ironed them when they were dry. We all celebrated when the washing machine arrived. It was electric but had a wringer that had to be cranked by hand. Semeha thought it was a wonderful innovation.

▲ ▲ ▲

We added to the joy of our summer with an August vacation of twenty-five days on the island of Cyprus, about a seven-hour flight from Cairo. We planned to travel from Cairo with an adventurous group of friends. The Stehn's were an AMOCO family that included Julie Stehn, Sonja's good friend. When we got to Cyprus, we would meet Bud Dodge, his wife, Diane, and their daughter, Deirdre, Troy's preschool friend. Bud was the CAC physical education teacher and coach.

We bought our tickets at a travel agency in Cairo, paying in Egyptian pounds. We planned to withdraw US dollars from our Bank of Denver account to pay for our lodging, food, and some purchases. Egyptian pounds were "soft currency," useless outside of Egypt, so we had arranged for Floyd's dad to wire five hundred dollars from our account in Denver to a bank in Nicosia, Cyprus. We were told there wouldn't be any problem in transferring funds from the Denver bank to the Bank of Cyprus.

After arriving at the airport in Cyprus, we went to the designated bank in Nicosia, the capital. They had no record of any transfer of funds. What to do next? Unfortunately, it was impossible to pick up a telephone and make an international phone call. We needed to contact Floyd's father. We hadn't heard from the Shoemakers for several weeks and surmised that they were on vacation, so a very friendly Cyprus Bank officer helped us cable my mom and dad who, in turn, would locate Floyd's parents to get the details.

The same day we sent the cable, a message came from Floyd's dad telling us he had sent a five-hundred-Egyptian-pound check to the Bank of Port Said, Cairo, Egypt. We were horrified! We had asked for a five-hundred-American-dollar check to be sent to the Bank of Cyprus—a further complication. There was no International Bank of Port Said in Cairo; however, there was a Bank of Port Said in Cyprus, but they had received no check yet. There was also an International Bank of Port Said in Port Said on the Suez Canal, but no one was allowed there anymore except the Egyptian military. With much advice from our travel companions and the Cypriot Bank people, we cabled Floyd's dad, asking him to stop payment on the check, which might be impossible, and cable five hundred to the Bank of Cyprus. In the meantime, the bank loaned us some money, so we could get to our destination in Kyrenia, where we had reservations for three weeks. God bless the helpful Cypriot banker.

I couldn't wait to tell my parents about this beautiful island and its friendly people.

▲ ▲ ▲

August 5, 1972

Cyprus seems like seventh Heaven—the food is delicious, everything is sparkling clean (not a fly or mosquito), and the combination of blue, blue ocean, and wooded mountains in Kyrenia is truly lovely. Kyrenia is just a village with a small harbor full of all kinds of boats. The town is built around an old Crusader castle. Our British-owned apartment building sits above the castle and is just a few hundred feet from the sea that we view from our front balcony. The rear balcony looks out onto the Kyrenia Mountains. Everything in the apartment is furnished: the refrigerator and cupboard are full of supplies. The furniture is carved wood in a simple Cypriot style. We've been cooking breakfast and lunch and a few dinners. A large grocery store in town has all kinds of goodies—delicious butter, cheese, and milk products, even Campbell bean with bacon soup, canned pineapple, peanut butter, Jell-O pudding, real Coca-Cola, and Missy's favorite candy bars, all products we haven't had for a year. We're having an eating orgy ...

The sea is great fun, even for me with my limited swimming ability. Troy adores it. We got together with the other two families and rented two boats yesterday, went around the coast, dropped anchor, and swam. The kids used swim masks and snorkels, so they could just float on their stomachs and see the colored fish in the clear water ...

▲ ▲ ▲

Our money came to Nicosia without a problem, so the Stehns drove us into Nicosia to pick it up. While we were there, we did some shopping for next year. We brought one empty trunk to fill with purchases. Our next task was to rent a Land Rover for two weeks, big enough to hold all the kids in our two families plus some of Bud

Dodge's family, who had been there all summer. Having a friend to arrange housing and show us historic sites was very helpful. We spent our last week in Cyprus touring some intriguing castles in the mountains near Kyrenia. We climbed hundreds of steps up a mountain to visit Buffavento, a crusader castle built in the 1100s. The view of the mountains and the sea was the climax of our efforts.

The American Embassy in Cyprus also provided us with health check-ups, a welcome service that our understaffed embassy in Cairo couldn't provide. Everyone was healthy, and the kids were thriving. Sonja and I would both need some dental work when we returned, but we knew of a good dentist trained in the US. I also had my annual Pap smear while I was there. A Navy doctor at the embassy sent the smear to Bethesda, Maryland for analysis, and the results came to me in Cairo two months later, a round-about means of accomplishing this, but it worked. Floyd had gained about eight pounds, thanks to the Greek food and the sea-side relaxation.

We were already talking about coming back to Cyprus in December. Cyprus Air would give us half-price tickets during the Christmas season, so the airfare in Egyptian pounds was not a problem. We had to decide whether to spend money from our shrinking US bank account. We lost money each month on the house we owned in Eaton Rapids, Michigan because the renters were going through a divorce and were three months behind in the rent. The management company had some prospects interested in renting, but the renters would not allow him to show the house. An eviction notice was in the works, but we still needed to retrieve the rent we were owed. We were told an attorney friend of ours would bring legal action against the renters. Hopefully, a Christmas trip to Cyprus was still a possibility.

▲ ▲ ▲

We were back in our villa by the end of August. I thought it would be a shock to get back, but things in Ma'adi looked pretty and green, and the villa was lovely. The house, Patches the Cat, and two recently acquired parakeets were still alive when we returned. Salim said he had been at the house each day protecting it and the pets. Sonja and Missy started school on Monday, September 4, and Troy's preschool started that week too. I taught journalism three days a week and technical writing to Egyptian geologists at GUPCO twice a week—fun jobs and not too time-consuming. I had time to write poetry and a few feature articles requested by the *Cleveland Plain Dealer* and the *Michigan State Journal*. Kit Miniclier, the Associated Press bureau chief, mentioned the possibility of writing feature articles for AP too.

Soon after we returned, Sonja and Missy dressed up for an end-of-summer party at the Ma'adi Club. The party was for kids from fourth to eighth grade, but parents and little kids also joined in the fun as the evening wore on. The club had a large tile dance floor under trees lit by small lights. Music was provided by a small band in addition to an Egyptian disc jockey with tapes of dance music.

▲ ▲ ▲

A full year had passed quickly. We had experienced the pain of homesickness, Floyd's near-death bout of cholera, the warning signs of a possible war, and all the stages of culture shock. We had also found friendships with foreign correspondents, local journalists, Russian diplomats, Egyptologists, and locals from every walk of life—people we would never have had the chance to know in the US. I had new and interesting jobs, and the children were getting an outstanding education. Our lives were rich with wonderful experiences so, like any good editor, I continued to delete the elements that might be frightening, not just from my parents' letters, but most of the time, from my own mind.

September marked the arrival of twenty-four new American University families on a TWA charter flight. We were asked to host a family to help them get acquainted with life in Ma'adi and assist with any problems they might have. What wisdom had we gleaned in this past year that we could impart to a new family? We would see.

Ma'adi Dawn

Ma'adi dawn is a donkey's bray
a noisy, raucous eye-opening day
unfolding with electronic prayer
that echoes, vibrates on Nile-borne air.

Staccato notes from the rooster choir
sound from rooftops and dung heap mire.
They rise as one to shout their praise
like soccer fans on holidays.

Crows in casuarina trees
dive-bomb doves with a screechy wheeze
while radios tune to some Om Kalthoum
blending noise with a half-tone croon.
The sun can't sneak from Moqqattam
unheeded and without sala'am.

9

The Accident

IT WAS ABOUT three-thirty on a hot September day—time for Sonja and Missy to be bicycling home from school. Troy was taking a nap after a swimming lesson at the Maadi Club. I was at the typewriter when the phone rang. It was Nancy Cronen, the mom of Liz, one of Missy's friends.

"Connie, you need to come right away. Missy has had a bicycle accident out in front of our house. Her leg looks like it might be broken. You may need to get a doctor. We don't know what to do. Please hurry."

The Cronens lived about five blocks from us. I told Salim what I was doing and asked him to watch Troy, as well as let Sonja know where I was when she got home from after-school basketball. I wheeled the bike out of the gate and took off as quickly as I could. My heart was beating faster than I could pedal. Thoughts collided in my mind: *How bad is this? Will we need a doctor? A hospital? How will I get Missy to the hospital? Nancy doesn't drive. God, please keep me strong!*

When I got to the Cronen's house, Nancy was waiting at the door. She took me into the living room where Missy was lying on a sofa. Missy was choking on her tears and clutching her upper leg.

"My leg hurts so much, Mom!"

I knelt on the floor next to the sofa and cradled her head. Her right leg appeared to be somewhat twisted. It was covered with road dust and scraped in several places but not bleeding. Her bike had been pulled inside the gate of the house. Nancy told me that another CAC student, a fifth-grade boy, was teasing her and rammed his

110

bike into hers. I switched from shock into emergency mode. What to do?

"We can't move her. We need a doctor and probably a hospital," I said, remembering Floyd's horrific trip to the maternity hospital in October.

"Maybe I should call the university for help finding a hospital."

Nancy told me to wait because she knew an Egyptian doctor who spoke English and lived in the neighborhood, so he might be able to examine Missy and decide what to do. Luckily, she was able to reach him. He came quickly, knelt down beside her, and gently moved her leg. She screamed in pain.

"Don't worry, little lady," he said. "I'll give you something for pain, and we'll get your leg all fixed."

The doctor suspected she had a broken femur in her upper right leg. He gave her a shot of morphine for the pain and called ahead to the hospital he was affiliated with. His colleague Dr. Grace, an orthopedic surgeon and professor at Cairo University, would be waiting for us. Now I was confronted with how to get her to the hospital. In the States, I would have called 9-1-1 for an ambulance. This service didn't exist in Cairo. No one with a car was available, so a taxi was the only option I could think of. Nancy called the local taxi stand and asked for the first available one.

A small Fiat cab arrived in ten minutes. The doctor carried Missy to the taxi as gently as possible and helped to prop her up with her leg flat on the back seat. I crouched on the floor between the seats, so I could comfort her with my arms and protect her leg on the ride. It seemed like an endless trip to the hospital, but when we arrived, Missy was carefully placed onto a gurney, and we were ushered inside. Dr. Grace, a British Egyptian trained in London, was waiting. He was kind and comforting.

While I was in the waiting room, I asked if I could use a telephone to call Floyd at the university, so he could join me at the hospital. When I explained what had happened, his response was unexpected.

"Oh, Connie. That's terrible. I hope she's doing all right. I'll see you at home after I finish some paperwork here."

"Do you mean you can't come now?"

"No, that's too complicated. I'll try to get home early."

Would his calm response have been different if I had been more emotional? If I had been crying? I wasn't one to cry until a crisis was over. *That relief might come tonight,* I thought. Recently I had observed that Floyd seemed to have limited emotional responses, very little fight-or-flight reaction to the everyday ups and downs that occurred in our family lives. Something was not quite right. He listened to our daily stories around the dining room table but rarely offered anything about his own campus life. Ignoring the bumps in life had always been a means of coping and protecting himself. I was frustrated with the lack of communication. I wanted to share the events in both our lives.

I just said, "OK, I guess I'll see you at home." I hung up the phone.

Two hours later, Missy emerged in a wheelchair with a white plaster cast that extended from the middle of her chest to the length of her injured leg. She would be unable to walk in this cast, which, I was told, would come off in four to eight weeks. We would return for X-rays and an examination in about four weeks. The hospital arranged for a Mercedes taxi to take us home to Ma'adi, so Missy could be stretched out in the back seat. At this point, she was groggy but able to talk about the accident.

"I don't know why he ran into me. Was he just teasing and didn't mean to hit me with the bike?"

Salim and Floyd met us at the gate when we got home. Floyd managed to carry Missy upstairs with Salim's help. They carefully placed her onto her bed, where she was greeted by Troy, Sonja, and Patches.

The gifts and well-wishes came flooding in. Our Egyptian friends, Shahinaz and Saleh, brought her a tape recorder, and Dale Compton, the minister, loaned her a small TV to watch the few shows produced in English. Oil company and embassy friends gave her an array of American treats: candy bars, popcorn, and brownie mixes, all from their precious stores of "privileges." The boy who had caused the accident brought her a large box of chocolates and an apology. I was hoping his parents had punished him for his carelessness. Her fourth-grade teacher planned lessons Missy could do at home.

Floyd was experiencing back problems, so Salim would carry Missy downstairs—stretched out straight like a platter of fresh fruit—so she could prop herself up on the sofa and eat supper with us. He would also carry her into a grassy area of the garden to lie on a blanket and get some fresh air and sunshine. Troy entertained her on the bed by racing his Matchbox cars on the plastic track that ran across her cast. Using the tape recorder was a favorite pastime, to record the voices of friends and family, but—more importantly—to play popular tape music from school friends. She and Sonja listened to some of their favorite songs. Simon and Garfunkel's "Cecilia," the Rolling Stones's "Angie," and Alice Cooper's "School's Out for the Summer" resonated throughout the villa. Despite all the restrictions of the cast, Missy maintained her usual positive attitude. What a trooper she was!

Our friends, Bill and Anne Marie, were long-term residents of the Middle East. They worried about the medical procedures in Cairo hospitals. They asked for permission to send Missy's X-rays to the university hospital in Beirut, known for its exceptional medical staff. Within a week, the hospital informed Bill that the position of the femur and the casting procedure met the highest standards.

When both sets of grandparents read the letter that informed them of Missy's accident, Floyd's father immediately asked us to send both Missy and Sonja home to Colorado.

▲ ▲ ▲

Thanks for your offer, Grandad, to fly the girls home. We'd all love to hurry home right now, but it's only a little more than five months until we can leave. We have a rather full, busy, and interesting life here with lots of obligations we need to fulfill. I must admit there would be more entertainment for Missy in the States and probably a home-bound teacher for lessons, but, as it stands, we're getting along fine. We have so many friends here now, Egyptian, American, and British, who have been supportive during this time. We appreciate your concern and look forward to seeing you this summer ....

▲ ▲ ▲

We hoped for positive results when Missy's four-week appointment came. Although we were disappointed, we understood the wisdom of the decision to keep on the cast. X-rays of the leg showed that it was healing properly and quickly but was not yet strong enough to stand on. Dr. Grace, who was very cautious, wanted her to remain in the cast for another four or five weeks. He said two and a half months is the usual period to be "off the leg" and in a cast, excluding a time of adjustment after the cast is taken off. This was tough news for long-suffering Missy, although she maintained a good attitude. We postponed a Christmas vacation trip but looked forward to returning to Cyprus or to Beirut during February's spring break.

▲ ▲ ▲

Four weeks passed slowly for Missy, but it was finally time to return to Dr. Grace. I waited outside the exam room while the X-rays were taken and reviewed. Dr. Grace stepped out to announce that everything looked perfect. The femur had healed nicely. He would remove the cast with a saw and examine the leg, and she could begin walking with a cane. No physical therapy was suggested, just the exercise of using the leg. Because the muscles had atrophied during the long period of activity, it would take several months to fully rebuild strength and flexibility. I heard the noise of sawing through the plaster cast, and then I heard Missy scream. A nurse came out and told me everything was all right. The doctor had lifted Missy's leg and bent it at the knee to break the scar tissue. She would never forget this final chapter in her recovery. But wait! There was another chapter to come.

▲ ▲ ▲

Missy started to recover, but her leg was still pale white and as thin as her cane. It was shocking to see the contrast between her legs. We massaged the leg with lotion daily, and she kept walking to build some muscle power. One morning, when I was helping Troy get dressed for preschool, I folded his pajamas to put into the bottom drawer of the dresser. Missy had just entered the room, walking with her cane. I opened the drawer and reached in with the pajamas. I touched something warm and moist. It squealed. I had startled a mother rat who had built a nest among the clothes.

I screamed. The rat jumped out. Missy was startled and tried to run out of the room but fell down and crawled out instead. I yelled for Salim to come upstairs and get the rat. He came into the room with one of his sandals in his hand. If he could catch the rat, which was now under the bed, he was going to clobber it with the sandal.

"You'll never catch the rat, Salim. Let's put Patches into the room. She'll find the rat and kill it!"

We closed the bedroom door but couldn't find the cat. Salim came back with a broom and managed the situation by quietly stalking the rat into a corner, leading to its demise. He carried the dead rat out of the room by its tail. Evidently, the rat had crawled up the drainpipe outside Troy's open bedroom window and found a good spot in an open drawer to have her babies. With the excitement over, Missy chalked up the event as part of her daily exercise.

▲ ▲ ▲

A contingent of new faculty members had arrived for the fall semester. We were AUC's designated friendship family for Dr. Robert and Joyce Ferrar from Cleveland, Ohio. Bob had a doctorate in political science and would join Floyd's department. The Ferrars had four children: Corey, Jason, Paul, and Brian. The three youngest children were biracial adoptees and all under six years old. Corey was barely two years old and added to the family just recently. Brian was a biological son and a pre-teen. Joyce had begun doing pioneering work for the adoption of "hard-to-place" children in Ohio, focusing on older, handicapped, and biracial children or members of sibling groups. Their family was an example of this work. It was unusual enough for us to bring our three young children to Egypt but extremely rare for the Ferrars to sign up for a stint at AUC with a newly adopted child and two other biracial kids in a country where adoption outside the family was unacceptable. They lived in a villa not far from ours, assisted by Amel, an Egyptian nanny who was also a household helper. As a friendship family, we couldn't have chosen a better match than the Ferrars. They would become our lifelong friends.

Floyd offered to get Bob started on his cultural journey by accompanying him on the train to the campus. Bob wanted to experience all of Cairo's people, not just the mid- to upper-class students at the university. With this goal in mind, they edged their way into a second-class car with standing room only. Bob was dressed for the first day of the semester in a crisp white shirt and a new tie he had purchased in Paris. He carried his favorite leather briefcase. The car was overflowing with passengers: a woman with a crate of live chickens balanced on her head, other women in black *melayas* with babies tucked close to their chests, street kids, day laborers, and students with their book bags. It was, in general, a true slice of Egyptian life. It was the proverbial can of sardines. There was no room to lift their arms, so Bob and Floyd placed their briefcases onto the floor between their feet. Bob was pressed up against a young boy who was just tall enough to fit under his chin.

Unfortunately, the kid was sneezing. They reached their university stop and managed to emerge with a crowd of people. What a relief! Bob looked down at his new tie. It was covered in snot from the little boy's nose. *Ma'alesh*. Just a typical train ride to work.

▲ ▲ ▲

Floyd unwittingly introduced Bob to another aspect of the Cairo street scene. The walk to the campus included the shoeshine man who greeted Floyd each morning. Floyd had an innate kindness and an inability to say "no" to any sales pitch. At least once a week, he would give the shoeshine man a few *piastres* to polish and buff his shoes. Bob needed a buffing after his train experience. On this particular day, the shoeshine man polished their shoes and gave them an extra benefit. He offered them a puff on his special pipe. They walked away with shiny shoes and a pleasant, giddy feeling.

Cairo Bus

People maggots swarm
the near-dead bus
as it limps down
Asr el Aini Street,
its right side crippled
by hanging riders.
Its missing windows
frames for Picasso-melted
commuters.

10

To Go or to Stay?

CHRISTMAS COOKIES AND Kool-Aid. What could be more tempting to four kids under five? Joyce brought her favorite cookies, adapted to use Egyptian ingredients, and I provided the grape Kool-Aid, a gift from my mom. The children were a beautiful mix of backgrounds: Corey, with curly blond hair and coffee-with-cream skin; Paul, with kinky black hair, deep brown skin, and green eyes; and Jason, with black hair, brown skin, and Korean features. Joyce and Amel, their nanny and housekeeper, had accompanied the group. Floyd was at home recuperating from a suspected ulcer diagnosed last week by an AUC physician. His diet was limited to soft foods and cow's milk. Salim had found a source of unpasteurized milk that he had boiled and cooled. Despite medical issues, Floyd remained committed to his career.

Salim brought the Kool-Aid and some dates and nuts to the table on the patio. Amel joined Salim in the kitchen for tea. After the treats, the kids dispersed to different areas of the house and garden. Jason raced cars with Corey in Troy's room, and Paul and Troy went frog hunting in the garden. It wasn't long before we smelled smoke and heard Salim yell and race out the back door.

The mound of dry leaves around the high hedge of poinsettia trees was burning and igniting the branches of the hedge. Troy and Paul had found a small firecracker left over from Ramadan and had somehow set fire to it. Floyd jumped up immediately and ran outside. He tried to stamp out some of the fire, but Ayoub was already there with his garden hose. He recruited the gardeners from the Turkish villa across the street and our German neighbor's house

119

next to us. They strung their hoses into our garden and started putting out the fire. Troy and Paul huddled together on the front step. Floyd lifted Troy up from the step.

"Did you do this, Troy?"

"It was a boomer, Daddy. Paul brought it over. We didn't think it would burn, just go bang."

Floyd gave Troy several hard swats on his behind, the first and only spanking Troy had ever had, and told him to go upstairs to his bed. Troy remembers the punishment to this day and, I think, relished the attention at the time.

This also marked the time when I lost the identity of *Om* Troy and became *Om* Sonja, the mother of my oldest daughter. Evidently, Salim had asked Amel about the children of mixed races who were visiting us. She told him they were adopted, just like Troy. This was news to Salim. Muslims believe that an adopted child, one not biologically related to the mother, does not qualify for the title of *Om,* mother. This distinction comes from Islamic principles of lineage and inheritance. In Islam, maintaining a clear lineage is important for legal, social, and religious reasons. Adopted children are not regarded as part of the biological family line; instead, they retain their original family name and identity, as prescribed by Islamic law. This new knowledge about Troy did not change Salim's affection for him.

▲ ▲ ▲

Our friendship with the Ferrars in their first few months made us realize how much we had learned since we arrived with the new AUC faculty almost fifteen months ago. It also made clear how much more we had to contribute and experience. Our two-year contract would end in June, when AUC would pay for our airfare back to the States. If Floyd wanted to find a job in the States for next September, he would need to begin his search immediately. We began considering another option: renewing his contract for another two years. Floyd's program was beginning to grow and thrive, but there was more work needed to stabilize it. An argument against staying in Cairo was my concern for his health. I was worried about the medical issues he had experienced and wanted him to have the best care possible. However, he trusted the doctors who had treated him here and didn't believe this was a good reason for leaving AUC.

I was personally in agreement for two more years. I had a fulfilling life with the family, some interesting teaching jobs, and my writing, with a particular focus on exploring the lives of the strong women I met, both Egyptian and expatriate. I had left behind the shyness of an only child and the lack of confidence I had when I first started to teach many years ago. It was a career I never would have chosen if Floyd hadn't needed the financial support to finish his professional education. I had taught eighth grade English, advanced high school creative writing and yearbook, GED, and a college course for engineering students. I had organized relocations to other houses or cities. My skills and strengths were growing, but I wasn't there yet. I still had those two a.m. I'm-not-sure-I-can-do-this doubts.

I had more to learn, and the Cairo experience had more to teach me. Floyd was occupied with his goal of establishing a graduate program in communications, so I had to develop my inner resources to make good family decisions and handle the challenges of daily life. More importantly, Sonja, Missy, and Troy were thriving and absorbing the new culture and language. They had more to learn and experience. They weren't yet ready to leave their lives in Egypt.

Another consideration in our decision to leave or stay for another two years was the fact that we had moved our family to six different houses in several cities in the past five years. We needed stability. After Floyd received an MA in journalism from the University of Missouri, he and I happily returned to Colorado State University, where he was hired to teach journalism, and where I was a graduate assistant while completing my MA. Sonja and Missy were born during the next five years. Then our family of four temporarily left the house we had built and moved to Dimondale, Michigan, for two years while Floyd took a leave of absence from CSU to begin work on a PhD at Michigan State. The next move was back to Colorado to resume teaching. When Sonja and Missy were six and seven years old, we adopted Troy and moved to a larger home in Ft. Collins.

Next came a move to finish up the PhD, so it was back to Michigan for our family of five to live in Eaton Rapids where I had a teaching job. What next? American University in Cairo. Sonja and Missy identified the moves by referring to the White House, the Red House, the Blue House, the Apartment, and now the Villa.

We involved the children in our decision-making process. They confirmed the positive experience of their lives in Cairo. They wanted to stay. Our decision was made. We would continue our lives in Cairo for another two years with the summer in between spent in Colorado.

As I reflect on this decision fifty years later, I shake my head at our audacity—our willingness to take risks as a family in Egypt. In those first two years, we had survived a bout of cholera, a broken leg, the daily physical risks of life in an overpopulated third-world city, and the mental stress of cultural adjustment. Would I do it again? Definitely! The Egyptian experience positively impacted our lives in ways that were not even imaginable then.

▲ ▲ ▲

In December, I wrote my annual Christmas letter to friends and family, a tradition I had started sixteen years ago as we made frequent moves back and forth from universities in Colorado, Missouri, and Michigan. It was a way to keep old friends as part of our lives.

▲ ▲ ▲

Cairo, Egypt, December 1972

Dear friends,

Christmas is in the air! Our experience of the past year in Egypt has taught us what signs of the season to look for. There are no Santa Clauses on street corners, no advertising on radio or TV in this Moslem country, and no snow-clad fir trees, but we still know Christmas is coming.

One of the first signs of the season was the blooming of the twelve-foot-high poinsettias that wall our villa. These brilliant blossoms are as common as the roses and carnations produced by the fruitful fields of winter and sold for just thirty piastres a bunch in the flower stalls in Cairo. The camel is another symbol of Christmas coming. During the winter months, small bands of camels are driven from the surrounding desert into the greenness of Maadi to graze. Some have even been seen nibbling on the bushes surrounding our villa. We will always be fascinated by these unusual animals. When we visited the camel market last month, we saw almost a thousand camels being sold for slaughter or as beasts of burden. The children, although a bit frightened by the huge, hobbled animals (one foot tied up one each), were intrigued by the rich Saudi Arabians bidding, with jewel-bedecked fingers, on a large white camel reputed to be one hundred years old. One white-robed Saudi even ventured a bid on Connie in her purple pantsuit.

Not only are the camels we see an everyday part of our landscape, but they also are symbolic of Egypt's involvement with the first Christmas and with the Holy Family when they sought refuge from the wrath of Herod. Just a few miles from where we live is the site where Mary, Joseph, and Jesus took shelter after crossing the desert into Egyptian Babylon, now known as Old Cairo. Reminders of history are with us every day as we drive along the Nile corniche and see the feluccas. Our trip down the Nile last winter showed us

123

the noble temples of Luxor and Karnak and the tombs of kings and queens with their detailed paintings and their atmosphere of peace and serenity. It also revealed the beauty of the Nile, harnessed by the dam at Aswan but still pursuing its course through the cataracts and many small islands dotting its path.

A variety of communities in Egypt are celebrating Christmas in their own traditional ways. We can enjoy the customs of our German, Russian, French, and Scandinavian neighbors. We plan to attend a mass at the Coptic Egyptian Orthodox Church and a typical Russian holiday with one of Floyd's students.

So far, our second year has been an active one, with none of the problems of adjustment we suffered the first year. Connie's progress with Arabic helped to solve some of the daily chores of transportation, handling servants, and shopping that plague families when they don't speak the language. Connie is teaching journalism and supervising the high school newspaper at the CAC, the school Sonja and Missy attend. She also teaches classes in technical writing to Egyptian geologists at one of the oil companies.

Floyd now has thirty-eight candidates for the new MA degree in mass communication, the graduate program he has initiated. Last spring, he was invited to participate in a seminar in Beirut on East-West communication, and this fall he spoke to the World Health Organization. His book, written with major professor Everett Rogers, was reviewed in an Arabic magazine in Cairo recently, so he now receives invitations to the Egyptian Writers' Club, where he can visit with the country's best-known novelists and journalists.

Sonja, now in middle school, particularly enjoys second-year French and her weekly ballet classes. She performed her first solo in June in a program in Cairo and received good reviews in English, French, and Italian newspapers. Melissa loves all the sports available in this year-round summer climate. She takes tennis lessons, competes in athletic programs in school, and swims daily during the warmer season; Troy, just four this month, loves his preschool

124

activities, is starting to swim like a fish, and dotes on our menagerie of animals at the villa.

We've learned one important thing from our stay here. Wherever it is celebrated, in the snowy winters of Michigan or Colorado, or the temperate climate of the Mediterranean, the message of Christmas is the same.

"I love," observes the squire in Washington Irving's The Sketch Book, *"to see one day in the year, at least, when you are sure of being welcomed wherever you go and of having, as it were, the world all thrown open to you."*

Kulli sana w'inta tayyib. *May every year find you well, and Merry Christmas!*

The Shoemakers

▲ ▲ ▲

December also brought shopping trips for small Egyptian souvenirs to send to our family when friends here traveled to the States and could mail them. A trip to the Mousky *suq,* a huge bazaar, was part of the holiday experience. Diane Dodge, former cheerleader and wife to the CAC coach, was my shopping partner. Diane was a sexy blonde whose fashion sense wasn't quite up to Cairene standards. Instead of wearing pants and tops with at least a short sleeve, she preferred skirts just below the knee and sleeveless blouses—which many Egyptians considered too much skin exposed to sex-starved men. Taxis had become our preferred means of travel because the packed train always exposed us to groping men, an experience that had made me so angry last time that I threaded a hat pin in my shoulder bag, all the better to poke any straying hands.

Diane and I met at the taxi stand in Ma'adi but couldn't find our usual driver, Saeed the Spy. We ended up with an unknown character named Ahmed, who muttered throughout the drive and continually readjusted the dangling prayer beads and a hula dancer in a grass skirt dangling from the rear-view mirror of the Fiat. His route to the Mousky was a different one than we were used to. We reminded him of our destination. In a few minutes, he came to an abrupt stop at the side of a crowded road near the City of the Dead.

"Istanna shwaya," wait a minute, he said. He got out, walked to a soft drink shop, and disappeared inside. The minute he told us to wait became five minutes. He didn't appear.

Residents living in the City of the Dead had to edge around the taxi to get to their destinations. They would tap on the taxi windows, wave and laugh. Diane and I weren't sure what to do. Should we get out and look for the driver? That didn't seem like a good idea in a place where foreign women were a novelty. Still no Ahmed. A large elderly woman in a black *melaya* was propped on a cane in front of the taxi as if she were protecting us. After a few more minutes, she came to the passenger door and opened it.

"Ahmed *xalas!*" she said and patted her chest. "I help."

The offer to help was welcome, but we didn't know if we could trust her. She closed the door and came back in a few minutes with another taxi following her. The driver got out to talk to us.

"*Amrikani?* Good people. I take you where you want to go."

We took the offer and got into his old Mercedes cab. A big tip was in order when we arrived at the Mousky. However, our adventure that day wasn't finished. I bought two cloth wall hangings that would be easy to send with Reverend Compton when he got to the States. Diane purchased a brass coffee server and a small tray. We stashed our purchases in the mesh bags we had brought with us and joined the crowd moving through the shops to the exit.

Suddenly Diane shouted, "Stop that, damn it! *Amshi*! Get away from me."

She swung her bag behind her, hitting a man with a cane—a blind man. Someone in the press of people behind us had given Diane a firm pinch on the butt. Obviously, it wasn't the blind man. With a quick apology to the blind man in English and Arabic, both of us hurried to the taxi stand and home to Ma'adi with our purchases and our frustrations in hand.

Diane and I approached cultural norms very differently. I tried to show respect for Muslim culture and smooth my way by dressing and behaving in ways that were appropriate. Diane took pleasure in challenging the norms and inviting attention. I must admit, however, partnering with her was never boring.

▲ ▲ ▲

December was made more festive with the celebration of Troy and Missy's birthdays on the third and the ninth. Troy would be four and Missy ten. We couldn't celebrate in Cyprus as we had planned, but we were so pleased with Missy's continued recovery that we added a little extra to our Christmas spirit. We discovered that we could rent movies and a man to show the film right in our own house. One of the kids' favorites, *Dr. Doolittle,* was our choice. More than a dozen friends of both Missy and Troy showed up to watch the movie in our living room and have birthday cake afterward.

Salim contributed to our Christmas celebration by finding us a tree. We came home from an excursion to the Hilton Hotel to find a five-foot cypress tree nailed to the parquet floor in the corner of our living room. He evidently went out the night before and cut down the tree from a nearby property. Dear, sweet Salim wanted to please us, even if it involved a minor theft and some damage to the parquet floor. All in all, the Christmas of 1972 was one to be remembered.

January Rain

I hurry home past carts
heaped high with cauliflower
as singsong showers hush
the haggling of the suq.

It's a birthday, this rain,
celebrated once each year
christening the dusty leaves
from grayness into glistening green
daubing poinsettias with drops
that liquefy the crimson blooms
blending on the palette of the street.
The sweeper with his switch
of twigs bends to his work
whisks up the swirling hues
restoring all to gray.

11

The School Next Door

"*BILADI, BILADI, BILADI*" was my reminder that it was 9 a.m. Time for school to begin in the government school next door. Sleepy young children in the courtyard began the day by singing the Egyptian national anthem, "My Countrymen, My Countrymen, My Countrymen." I could look down from our bathroom window and into the windows of one of the elementary-level classrooms. The windows had long since been free of glass, so the view was clear. The children shuffled, scrambled, and elbowed each other as they rushed into the room. Girls and boys were separated and seated in threes or fours in desks made for two. The *mudarissa*, a tall, heavy woman in a black *melaya,* sharply tapped her ruler on the desk. She moved in front of the desk to shout out the roll of names and receive homework from each student.

The children appeared to be about eight or nine years old. Each was dressed in a faded khaki-colored uniform: girls in long-sleeved dresses and boys in pants and shirts. I was fascinated as I watched each child come forward with what looked like a somewhat tattered, bound book.

"Ahmed!" she shouted. "*Alatool.*" Hurry up!

A little boy limped to the desk and showed his book to the teacher. She gave it a quick glance and shoved it against his chest.

"*Mish kwayiss!*"

Next came the ruler from the desk. She grabbed the boy's hand and slammed the ruler against his open palm. He started crying and pulled away. She grabbed his arm and hit him on the shoulder. A final blow came to Ahmed's head.

"My God! Stop that," I shouted, even though I knew she couldn't hear me from my second-floor window. Ahmed disappeared and the parade of children was finished. I considered what I could do. Continue to spy on the classroom? Just ignore the situation and not look out the window again? Go next door to talk to the headmistress? Would my Arabic be good enough? Would she shout at me and call me a crazy American?

I went downstairs to tell Salim what I'd just seen. He wasn't surprised or angered at my description.

"*Ma'alesh,* Madame. School not good."

After some thought and a few deep breaths, I decided to go next door. When I walked into the schoolyard on the other side of the dilapidated building, I saw a rather official-looking woman talking to a ragged suffragi. I asked if she was the headmistress, she stepped back, took a long look at me, and nodded her head. I introduced myself.

"*Ana mudarissa kaman.* I'm a teacher, too," I explained. With a combination of gestures and Arabic, I tried to explain what was happening in the classroom I could see from my window. She listened, nodded, and seemed to understand.

"*Mish kwayiss auwy, mudarissa ahu hinak,*" expressing her opinion of the very bad actions of the teacher on that side of the building. She finished with the comment that the teacher was *xalas,* finished. She surprised me with a thank you, and indicated the teacher would be strongly corrected.

The next day, I again looked down from my bathroom window. I saw that an old T-shirt had been fastened across the gaping space of the classroom window. I couldn't see inside, but I could hear the same *mudarissa* calling the names of the students to review their homework. I heard the slap of the ruler and the occasional cries of reprimanded students. The headmistress had covered up my view of the offensive teacher.

I was so frustrated at not being able to plant even a small seed of change in the ills that I saw every day. Salim was right to say "*Ma-alesh.*" It's not good, but that's the way it is. Acceptance was not easy, but it was just one of the lessons I learned in this school of Egyptian life.

▲ ▲ ▲

Our neighborhood was a capsule of the present and the past of the suburb of Ma'adi. Sadat's *infitah* policy initiated in 1972 encouraged foreign investment to widen the scope of the economy. The open-door policy was a departure from the more state-controlled economic practices of Gamal Abdel Nasser. It influenced Ma'adi by increasing its international population as it became a preferred location for expatriates working with multinational companies and other international entities. The villa of a Siemens representative was to our west behind another hedge. We could hear them speaking German but never saw them. Salim was acquainted with the cook and informed us it was just a husband and wife, no children. Siemens had a long history in Egypt dating back to the late nineteenth century. Now they were involved in telecommunications and electrical engineering projects.

Across the street from our villa were two other villas of about the same age and size as ours. One belonged to an aging Turkish couple. The gentleman wore the traditional red *tarboush* and walked with a cane. His wife was always clad in formal, go-to-tea dresses and pearls around her neck. I would see them once a week driving a polished black Daimler limousine of ancient origin. They would take the car out of their garage, drive around the neighborhood for ten or fifteen minutes, and carefully park it back in the garage. Although I never met them formally, whenever I saw the wife, she would say, "Good morning."

My guess was that they had come to Egypt sometime in the late 1950s, when Turkey and Egypt maintained embassies and consulate generals in each other's capitals.

The garden of the second villa was visible from our front gate. The kids loved to look at the American family's kiddy pool decorated with a Mickey Mouse caricature, a blue plastic pool that suggested a small child lived there. But instead of a playmate, the bather was a large, shaggy Newfoundland dog, who desperately needed to cool off in the hot Egyptian summer. We shook our heads considering why anyone would want to bring a Newfoundland to Cairo. Then we remembered how much we missed our dog, Taffy, and the two cats we had to leave behind in Eaton Rapids, Michigan. We, too, like the owners of the Newfoundland, always took our pet cats and dogs with us on each of our many moves in the United States.

Just a short walk down the back street from our garden was an impressive villa surrounded by a stucco wall. It was reported to belong to the Shah of Iran's wife, Queen Farah Pahlavi. The villa itself had historical significance. It was designed in the 1920s by Ariston St. John Diamant, a significant figure in the history of Egyptian architecture, and had been home to various notable figures before becoming associated with the Iranian royalty. It became the temporary residence of the King and Queen Pahlavi during their exile following the Iranian Revolution. The couple was hosted by Egypt due to their political situation and lack of refuge elsewhere. Queen Farah was an intriguing woman who trained as an architect in Paris and founded Iran's first American-style university, like AUC. The university enabled women to become students in Iran. King Reza Pahlavi died in exile in 1980. Queen Farah continued to live in exile, dividing her time between Paris and Washington DC.

In contrast to the Pahlavi villa, there was a two-story military building of unknown purpose to civilian passersby but protected by a shallow trench dug into the dirt roadway. Sandbags rimmed the front of the trench. It was staffed by two soldiers with rifles propped against the buttress. They would greet walkers with a "*Sabah el kheir*" while they casually drank their morning coffee.

One of Missy's favorite places was the nearby candy store, a tiny building managed by an English-speaking Egyptian. The store featured local sweets in addition to candies from England, Germany, and France but nothing from the United States because of the boycott. Missy's favorites were Nestle's chocolate bars and gumballs. One day, she was reaching into a large jar for some gumballs when she accidentally tipped it over. Gumballs scattered all over the dirt floor. Missy was horrified. The manager took her bicycle and chained it to a pole.

"If you want your bicycle, go tell your mother to come and pay me for the gumballs."

Missy did as she was asked. I settled the bill. Missy remained a good, now careful, customer.

▲ ▲ ▲

Our neighbors also included street people who sought *baksheesh* from the foreign families who lived in the villas. A regular visitor was a blind man guided by a little boy about eight years old. The little boy would open the gate and lead the blind man to the door, so he could tap on it with his stick. When I opened it, he would bow and scrape to me, the rich American madame of the household. He always asked for clothes or money. Each time they came, I gave them a few *piastres*. This encouraged them to come every few days. One day, I answered the door and found the little boy crying.

"No shoes. Foot bad," the blind man said, pointing to the little boy's mud-caked foot.

I promptly found an old pair of Missy's sneakers to give to the boy. They left with many *shukrans* and blessings. When they reached the gate, I saw the old man grab the sneakers from the boy and hit him over the head with them before he tucked them under his *galabiya*. Salim told me not to give anything to them again. He would chase them away. He also told me that some beggars would allow themselves to be blinded or be handicapped in some way to make a living from begging. I appreciated Salim's wisdom and followed his advice. I was struggling with the difficulty of making a difference in just one child's life. Was it truly impossible?

The most startling visitors to the neighborhood were two men from the Fayoum, an oasis about sixty miles south of Cairo.

One afternoon, Floyd was out in the garden with Troy, trying to pick a papaya that was too far above his head to reach. Normally, Ayoub, our dedicated gardener, would have been there to help, but he was at a clinic in Cairo today being treated for schistosomiasis, also known as bilharzia.

Ayoub had worked barefoot in the garden of this university villa for more than fifteen years. Water from the Nile was released to irrigate the garden twice a week. The water contained parasitic worms that came from infected animals and animal and human waste. The parasites could penetrate the skin of bare feet, enter the bloodstream, and migrate to the liver, intestines, and other organs. Ayoub had been suffering from the fever, muscle aches, and belly and joint pain of bilharzia for several weeks. Since he was hired by the university as a gardener, he was able to get medication for this condition. Salim knew about this benefit and encouraged him to get treated.

The absence of Ayoub didn't stop Floyd from retrieving the tempting papaya. Troy asked his dad to put him onto his shoulders, so he could grab the fruit. It worked! Two men on the road had been watching the procedure and clapped their hands in applause. They were equipped with long, forked sticks and two heavy cloth bags.

"See big snake in garden. Cobra!" one of the men said. "Bad, bad for little boy. We catch and kill snake for you. Only three pounds."

Floyd wasn't sure if this was just a ruse or if there was some reality to it. He asked Troy to fetch me from the house to see if I could find out more by using my Arabic. When I came out, one of the men said our neighbors had asked him to catch a snake in their yard, but it had come through the hedge and was somewhere in our garden. I knew there were several kinds of poisonous snakes in Egypt, and yes, there was even an Egyptian cobra, but what would a big snake be doing here? If Ayoub were here, he would verify to the men that there was no such snake in *his* garden. With an attempt at an Egyptian sense of humor, I decided to play along.

"Wow! A cobra is very bad. I'll give you two pounds to catch it, but I want to keep it when you find it, so I can show it to my friends."

"No. No, Madame. We show you snake and take snake away. You no keep."

I said I was sorry but it was no deal. If I paid two pounds, I got to keep the snake. We had a few more exchanges about the danger of ignoring the snake in our garden or letting them catch it, so our little boy would be safe. I finally ended the repartee.

Thank you so much," I said. "*Ma'asalama.* Goodbye."

The men shook their heads in unison. "Bad, bad, bad," they chanted as they turned away from the gate and started down the road. As they walked away, I noticed that one of the bags looked as if it was already full and something was moving inside.

Government School

The Nile-dipped dawn brings children
straggling down the street.
worn briefcases clutched tight
in khaki-covered arms.
They cluster like an army
whose battles have been long
then really in the courtyard
to shout their Biladi song.

"My name's Saeed.
I want to learn to count and read
and maybe even write my name,
so Baba will be proud of me.
My sisters cannot come to school.
Baba says they're just girls, you see."

The mudarissa clangs
the bell for classes to
begin and students shove into
the desks in threes
and sometimes fours, their elbows
welcoming the boy or girl next door.
The sing-song drill of lessons starts.

"My name's Saeed, teacher. I don't
know how to make that letter right.
The slate's so small; there is no light.
Oh, can't I ask one question more
without your scolding and your stick?
My hands already are so sore."

The drone of lessons fills
the school until the bell.
Then through the doors and windows
children burst like bombs.
They scuffle, scatter, scramble
tin the street
tossing their copybooks and
shouting to be free.

I'll say, "Baba, my day was fine,"
and not tell him about the room
with peeling paint and broken glass.
I'll hide the tear streaks and the shame
and show Baba my copybook,
where sometime I may write my name.

12

Spy vs. Spy

NO FIREWORKS AND rowdy celebrations on New Year's Eve. A blackout of Cairo and its suburbs, including Ma'adi, began at dusk. We could hear more than the usual whirring of helicopters above us and the low roar of Army trucks, yet people were still out strolling and having coffee in dark shops. It wasn't the beginning of war with Israel, but it was a rehearsal for what was to come soon.

Aside from war preparations, the entire month of January was marked by student protests, a time-honored tradition in Egypt. This period of strikes, sit-ins, and protests came after decades of student activism in the entire country. Cairo University, with a student population of approximately fifty thousand students, was heavily represented among the protesters. Public universities, like Cairo University, did not charge tuition fees, and students were often provided with additional support such as stipends or housing allowances. Free higher education in Egypt was largely subsidized by the government as part of broader socialist policies implemented under President Nasser. These policies aimed to promote social mobility and address inequality, but there was a problem. There was no work after completing university studies.

The students in Tahrir Square demanded that Anwar Sadat's government give them greater political freedoms, improved living conditions, participation in decision-making, more academic freedom, and a reduction in the influence of security forces on university campuses. President Sadat's response was expected. Riot police surrounded the crowds with tear gas and batons to prevent the protest from continuing. This reaction did not deter the student-led unrest. It continued throughout Sadat's presidency.

Egyptian students were not alone in their protests. In 1970, Ohio National Guard troops fired on unarmed students at Kent State university in Ohio protesting President Nixon's expansion of the Vietnam War into Cambodia. It became a defining moment for anti-war activism. Since then, the intensity of protests in the United States had considerably diminished. Anti-Vietnam War sentiment remained strong, but large-scale demonstrations had declined because of protest fatigue, the winding down of US troop involvement in Vietnam, and the signing of the Paris Peace Accords on January 27, 1973, which aimed to end direct US military involvement in Vietnam.

Floyd and Bob, good travel buddies by now, were somewhat limited in their trips to the university by the huge numbers of protesters in Tahrir Square. They took taxis instead of the train when necessary. AUC did not close its doors entirely. However, the university did face disruptions and challenges due to the ongoing protests and unrest. Despite occasional class suspensions due to external volatility, AUC stayed open and continued operations as much as possible.

As 1973 began, Sadat continued his efforts to make peace with Israel and to recover Egyptian territory lost in the last war. The strongest of these peace attempts had come in the summer of 1972 when the president expelled twenty thousand Soviet advisers from Egypt and opened new diplomatic channels with Washington DC, Israel's key ally. He hoped the US would be an essential mediator in any future peace talks. He also had formed a new alliance with Syria.

We were always cognizant of our parents' concerns for our safety as they read news reports of the turmoil in Egypt. We also felt the need to show them the unique experiences we were enjoying.

▲ ▲ ▲

February 11, 1973

It was wonderful to receive a recent Rocky Mountain News. *The Middle East news in the Rocky was surprising and much scarier than being here on the scene. Everything is quite calm here, with much criticism in Egyptian newspapers of the US support of Israel and America's position regarding the Middle East ...*

Life goes on in Cairo, and we continue to be fascinated by the once-in-a-lifetime experiences we can have. We went to the camel market on Friday—just like something out of Arabian Nights. They sell one hundred camels a day. Many camels come from Sudan with their drivers. Most of the camels were hobbled on one leg and hopping around on the other three legs. Can you imagine herds of hopping camels coming at you from all sides and clusters of Sheikhs wanting you to take their pictures?

This market is definitely not a tourist attraction, so the group of CAC teachers who went with us was the only group of non-Arabs. One of the marketeers told us that one can buy a camel anywhere from LE ninety to LE 275, depending on its condition. We saw one huge camel that was reputed to be one hundred years old and was priced at LE 275. Most of the camels were sold for slaughter, but some will be used as beasts of burden on the farms surrounding Cairo. While we watched wealthy Saudi Arabians with rings on every finger making bids on animals, Floyd got a bid for me for LE 175: about four hundred dollars, from a Saudi sheikh. (It must have been the purple pantsuit I was wearing.) I guess I should have been flattered.

We took Troy, Missy, and Karen—one of Missy's friends—with us. Sonja stayed home to swim at the Ma'adi Club. Troy was fascinated, although a bit afraid of the huge animals. He spent a lot of time above the fray on Floyd's shoulders. Missy and Karen were disgusted by being looked at and having their hair touched by the curious people at the market. It's hard for them to understand that we stare just as much at the Egyptians (but we don't touch them!)

Mostly it's Missy's blonde hair they want to touch. Her hair is even blonder and longer than when we arrived in Cairo.

Another intriguing, but somewhat unique, trip for the whole family was to the Giza Zoo, a well-established zoological garden begun by the Khedive Ismail in 1891. Unlike American zoos, in this one we were encouraged to feed the animals. I gave Troy a few piastres to hand to one of the zookeepers. He filled Troy's hands with a huge bunch of clover to give to a hippopotamus. Troy dropped the clover when the hippo opened its mouth too close to his face. The zookeepers kept a ready supply of all kinds of animal and bird feed. Just tip them and you could feed almost any animal. The tips supplemented the small salaries they made. Children could also have their photos taken with a lion cub or baby chimpanzee—or even with their heads inside the mouth of an elephant kept on a short chain. We said "no" to this experience. Cairo cats roamed through the zoo and in and out of the animal enclosures. These were just as interesting to our children as the zoo animals.

▲ ▲ ▲

One of the most endearing aspects of the culture was the jokes Egyptians told about themselves. This humor often served as a coping mechanism for the various challenges they faced in daily life, such as economic difficulties and traffic congestion. Even spy activities were the butt of both American and Egyptian humor. Everyone spied on everyone else. American expatriates employed in Cairo, including diplomats, military personnel, and intelligence officers, engaged in intelligence gathering to monitor the activities of both Russians and Egyptians. The US and Egypt were engaged in a complex geopolitical relationship, with the US monitoring Soviet and Egyptian activities and vice versa.

I particularly enjoyed this joke: An Egyptian spy and an Israeli spy meet at a bar. The Israeli spy says, "I know everything about your plans."

The Egyptian spy replies, "That's funny because I don't even know what our plans are!"

Floyd and I weren't important enough to be real spies but served as useful conduits of information about other Americans. One of Floyd's students, the only Russian studying at AUC, was Anatoly Elexandervovich. Tola had all the qualifications to be an ideal spy. He had been working for three years in Egypt for the United Nations as an interpreter during Russia's building of the High Dam in Aswan and on the Sudanese border in charge of correspondence reports.

When the AUC student newspaper, *The Caravan*, interviewed him, they wrote:

▲ ▲ ▲

... Anatoly is a true international figure. He does not fit the stereotype of a Soviet Russian. He is Western in his demeanor but deeply Russian in his thinking. He has benefited by freedom of choice in working and traveling, which gave him the opportunity to moderate his ideas in the light of other people's ...

Anatoly is a graduate of the College of Foreign Languages in Moscow, worked in the translation department of Western languages, studied journalism, and worked for Radio Moscow. If his headquarters in New York allows him to stay in Egypt, he wants to become a full-time student at AUC. Among the teachers at AUC, Dr. Floyd Shoemaker impressed him.

"He is not the kind of teacher who has an answer to every question, but he thinks along with you."

Anatoly intends to go back to Russia eventually to continue his studies until he gets his PhD and then realizes his dream, which is to write and become an international journalist.

▲ ▲ ▲

Tola and his wife became part of our social circle, inviting us to dinner with Russian embassy associates and to other vodka-drinking gatherings where we served as potential informants on more important Americans. Bill Harrison's Ford Foundation connection and his frequent travel to the US and Middle Eastern countries made him a suspect.

"How's Bill doing now? I haven't seen him on campus. Just wondered if he was traveling," Tola would ask Floyd.

In turn, Bill Harrison would ask about Tola's activities. "Has Anatoly introduced you to his embassy colleagues? I'm sure they'd have lots of questions about the US and our opinions about Russia."

We concluded they were spying on each other.

However, I wasn't sure about the expertise of our Ma'adi spy, Saeed the taxi driver. Missy, Sonja, and I had great fun with Saeed. Our weekly taxi trips to Sonja's ballet classes gave us the opportunity to play games with him. We would ask him to drop us off at the front door of the Hilton, supposedly to have lunch or meet someone.

"Are you meeting a friend? What time should I come back to pick you up?" he'd always ask.

I would tell him that I didn't know but would call the Ma'adi taxi number if we needed him. Then we would go through the front door of the Hilton and out the back door, hire another taxi, and go on to our destination. On one occasion, he appeared at the back exit of the Hilton just as we came out the door. We ducked inside and hid like three fugitives from the law. This little game gave us some power over the intrigue that occupied the city.

It was normal for foreign journalists to be the subject of wiretaps and other spying ruses. Kennett Love, a *New York Times* foreign correspondent and one of our favorite outspoken personalities, was suspected of spying. He was recognized throughout the city because his constant companion was his German shepherd, Mister, in a city that feared dogs. Kennett's camera was always tucked in his backpack. He was a guest lecturer in one of Floyd's AUC journalism classes. His arrest and quick release for suspicious photography made his lectures even more riveting and foreshadowed his ultimate expulsion from the country later in the year.

Kennett had covered the Suez Canal crisis in 1956 and wrote a book about it: *Suez: The Twice-Fought War*, published in 1969. While biding his time waiting for a new war, he was working on a new book, *The New Arab World: A Portrait of Modern Egypt*. An event Kennett was a participant in may have drawn a spy or two mixed in with the more than thirty people at the Kefren Pyramid in Giza.

The event was Kennett's wedding. He was marrying Melinda Reed, a daytime television star in New York. Melinda had attended the Baldwin School, Bryn Mawr, Pennsylvania, and Boston University. I'm certain this was the only society wedding held in the desert heat at the pyramids. Our minister, Reverend Dale Compton, officiated at the Episcopal ceremony. The ring bearer, with a wreath of jasmine blossoms around his collar, was Kennett's beloved German shepherd, Mister.

Zoo Story

Stray cats who live in the Cairo Zoo
pay calls upon the seals
to steal their fish,
stalk the ostrich on pretend safaris,
skirt their cousin lions, tigers,
to leap amongst the giant tortoises,
finding a tidbit here and there.
Shadows which slip
through the rusted bars.

13

Spring Rebirth

THE SIMPLE BEAUTY of springtime in 1973 Cairo was made even more striking by its contrast to the complexities of daily life for Egyptians. The influx of people from the countryside looking for work added to the already overcrowded city of an estimated six million residents. This resulted in housing shortages, a strain on schools, transportation problems, and an overwhelming demand for water supplies, sewage systems, and medical facilities. A significant portion of the population lived in poverty. No one even thought about environmental concerns like air pollution from industry and vehicle emissions or the inadequate waste management systems that led to sanitation issues. The tensions produced by the preparations for war added to these concerns. Despite all these problems, the Egyptians still laughed, enjoyed shouted arguments, drank their Turkish coffees, and pursued their everyday lives with resilience.

The Shoemaker family went on with our privileged everyday lives. We lived in an upper-class garden suburb and had servants, diverse friendships, fulfilling jobs, and good education for our children.

▲ ▲ ▲

Taxi windows were our portals to the real life of the city as we traveled back and forth between Ma'adi and the heart of the Arab world, as Cairo was frequently called.

"Hey, Mom, look! There's that weird tree."

Like clockwork, Missy or Sonja would announce our approach to the huge banyan tree that held court in the middle of the Corniche on our way downtown. Today, the whole family was on board for a taxi ride with the purpose of dropping Sonja off at ballet and then taking me to my first class teaching advanced English at the university while Missy and Troy visited Floyd's office.

The one-hundred-year-old banyan tree was as large as our villa. Its branches arched several hundred feet across the sparse grass and concrete strip that ran along the Nile, almost touching the top of our taxi. Hundreds of gnarled roots appeared to be hanging loose from the tree, but on closer observation, you could see that each root had firmly attached itself to the mother tree crisscrossing the trunk and each other like bulbous veins and arteries. The swollen roots of the trunk had buckled up the concrete, and the twisted branches had formed a huge canopy of dusty green leaves that shielded all the activities underneath from the blistering rays of the sun.

We could see a whole city of activity under this tree. Beggars often slept away the afternoon in its shade. It gave refuge to those reciting their five daily prayers and offered space to barbers who produced, like magic, a shop from a plastic bag—scissors, strop, and soap. *Ductor al sinan* (a dentist) was at the ready with pliers and alcohol. The tree also provided a graveyard for the bones of dented Mercedes taxis, while grease-gowned men tried to make them whole again. In the afternoon, when school was out, little boys in their rumpled gray *galabiyas* would climb and hide in its twisted branches. Salim had told the kids that their favorite tree was the home of *djinn,* ghosts and demon-like creatures, that would dance and sing in the tree at midnight. If you got too close to the banyan at midnight, the *djinn* would pull you in, make you part of the trunk, and never let you go. A good Halloween story to tell when we got back to the States.

We slowed to a stop as we neared Tahrir Square and the train crossing near the university. Two men crossed the street to the center island. One of the men had his arms under the shoulders of what looked like the bloodied body of a young boy. The other had his arm under the boy's bent knees. I was next to the street side window of the taxi and tried to discourage the kids from looking. I could see the blood spatters on the men's *galabiyas* as they carefully placed the crumpled body onto the concrete. A crowd gathered and someone produced some newspapers to cover the body. Our driver shouted out the window at a bystander to ask what had happened. He was told that the child had fallen from the back of a train, where he was trying to catch a free ride. The crowd quickly dispersed and went on their way. We continued to the university. No ambulances, no emergency help, just a body under the newspaper. *Insha Allah,* God willing, someone would retrieve it. It was difficult to process that scene. It will remain in my mind forever.

▲ ▲ ▲

Back at the villa, there was another life. It was still springtime, and I needed to drink in all the beauty I could possibly swallow. Troy's play date with Justin provided the opportunity for him to ride his Big Wheels and for me to walk the tree-lined roads to his friend's house. I retrieved Troy from the kitchen, where he was having his almost daily tea with Salim (mostly sugar and milk). I noticed that Salim had given him a piece of sugar cane to chew on. I told both Salim and Troy that this was forbidden because it was bad for teeth. It was hesitantly thrown into the *zibala*. We told Salim where we were going and headed for the door.

"Look at my muscles, Mommy," Troy said as he pulled open the heavy villa door. Amazingly, we never felt the need to lock it.

Troy stopped under the portico in front of the door to look up at the high ceiling.

"Where's Izzy?"

"Izzy only comes out at night when the porch light is on," I responded. "She can catch the bugs that fly around the light."

After overcoming our initial apprehension, we welcomed Izzy the lizard into our menagerie. She was about two feet long, counting her tail, and had been part of the villa for many years, according to Ayoub. Also near the door was my favorite member of the villa garden, Snoopy, the villa dog. She came to greet me with a wagging tail. Her white and brown coat was looking healthier after my applications of medicated cream. When we first moved in, she was plagued by mange and ticks. Floyd, ignoring my warnings, picked off the ticks with his bare hands, part of his foolhardy ranch experience as a child.

Troy continued to show me his muscle strength by proudly opening the challenging latch on our garden gate, which was now covered with jasmine's white star-shaped flowers. The scent was delicious—not too sweet but still heady. Troy was pedaling his Big Wheels, so our progress was slow enough to enjoy the display of blossoming trees in various shades of pink, white, and purple. Sonja had checked out a flora and fauna book for me from the CAC library, so I could give names to the beauty I saw each day. Naming made these trees and flowers even more enticing.

On today's walk, we saw almond trees' delicate pink flowers and jacarandas flaunting purple-blue flowers that bloomed in clusters. My favorite was the plumeria tree with waxy five-petal blossoms of varied colors: white, pink, yellow, and even red. Almost all of the villas and buildings we passed were sand-colored, providing a good backdrop for the riot of colored blossoms from the trees, bushes, and plants. I was amazed when I spotted tulips and daffodils just starting to open their petals, probable descendants of the Europeans who originally lived in the villas. Blossoms of bougainvillea climbed up and over any obstacles on many of the villa balconies, ours included.

Troy needed a breather from his pedaling, so we stopped in front of a house with a huge veranda lined with potted oleander plants. The star-shaped, salmon-colored blossoms of oleander plants reminded me that this was my Grandmother Grondahl's favorite plant. In May, she would take it from their little house in Longmont, Colorado and put it on the front porch. When nights got cold, she would lug the heavy pot inside the side door to the living room and hide it from my grandpa's view because he didn't believe outdoor plants should be indoors. That plantwas still alive when we last visited my grandpa and grandma.

The combination of blooming trees and flowers brought back memories and created new ones. It provided a haven for me. I was transported away from the challenges we faced each day. We were still newcomers but felt more at home. We had integrated and adjusted our behavior, so it meshed more smoothly with Egyptian culture. We still had occasional bouts of anger when confronted with the complexities of life as foreigners but could usually find humor in most situations.

The most anger-invoking incidents related to Missy, Sonja, and my gender. Floyd led a protected life as a male. Light-skinned females with faces and hair exposed and who dressed to show too much skin were a magnet to some ill-mannered men. Even though the girls and I dressed conservatively, we sometimes suffered unwanted attention. My friend Shahinaz told me Egyptian women also would be sexually harassed if they drew attention to themselves by riding public transportation or walking in some areas of the city.

A woman riding a bicycle on the street with Egyptian men was a perfect situation for an encounter. One afternoon, when I was biking to Gomaa Brothers Grocery, I passed a cyclist standing on the roadside with his *galabiya* tucked up around his waist to facilitate his riding. When he saw me, he got on his bike to ride beside me, laughed, and pulled out his penis to expose himself. This made me so mad that I responded by laughing and pointing derisively at the offensive organ.

"*Kusumik!* F**you!" I said.

Luckily, he continued down the street, and I quickly turned into the row of Ma'adi stores. I had never, in Arabic or English, used that word. I must admit it felt good.

Missy later told me nonchalantly that, on their way to school with friends, they passed a man who, almost every day, stood on his apartment balcony and exposed himself.

I hadn't fully recovered from my episode with the perverted cyclist when I had to greet some American visitors. We had invited Dr. Meier, a Michigan State professor of philosophy, and his wife to dinner at our home. They were visiting Cairo on a tour. Dr. Rogers, Floyd's major professor, had arranged for them to meet us at the Sheraton Hotel, where they were staying. Before I called their room, I bought an old *Time* magazine to see what was happening in Cairo from an American perspective. After our greetings and a short get-acquainted chat, we went outside to get into a Mercedes taxi hailed by the Sheraton doorman.

"Welcome, *Ahlan! Amtikani? Faransawi?*" the driver asked as he opened the front door for Dr. Meier.

I explained in Arabic that I was American, not French, and that I had lived in Cairo for a long time. I told him in Arabic where I wanted to go. He shook his head in agreement and seated himself in the cab. I opened the rear door, and Mrs. Meier and I settled into the back seat.

Before we pulled away from the curb, I asked the driver how much the ride would be.

"*Arbaa sinen,* Madame. Just four pounds," he replied.

"*La! Mish kwayiss.* Ma'adi one pound fifty."

He started the car and set the meter at two pounds.

"*Istanna Shwaya!* Wait a minute!" I pointed at the meter.

His reply was, "Ma'adi long, long way, Madame!"

I'd had it. I took my *Time* magazine, rolled it up, and swatted him on the back of his head. I got out of the car and motioned to the doorman. I told him what had happened. He said he would report the driver to the tourist police. The somewhat shocked Meiers got out of the taxi and into another taxi called by the doorman. We were on our way to Ma'adi for one pound fifty.

"Do you have to do this every day?" Mrs. Meiers asked.

"No," I replied, "Just today is enough."

▲ ▲ ▲

That was Cairo! This was Beirut, the Paris of the Middle East. A spring respite from the stresses of Cairo was a long-planned trip to Egypt's close neighbor, Lebanon. The Ferrar family joined us for the trip. Thanks to bargain airfare on Middle East Airlines, children younger than twelve flew half-price. And we had five of these! That extra cash gave us what we needed to rent a nice hotel on a high point overlooking the Mediterranean.

Beirut had a vibrant culture, cosmopolitan atmosphere, and bustling nightlife. Its population was only 475,000, compared to Cairo's five million people. Also, unlike Cairo, its liberal atmosphere attracted both intellectuals and tourists. Favorable banking regulations made it an international financial hub with banks from around the world. Floyd had spent time at the conference last year at a combined casino and hotel high in the mountains overlooking the city, but he had experienced none of the city life.

The children discovered that the city was a shopping paradise, offering a mix of traditional *souks* and, most importantly, modern shopping centers. Upscale boutiques were spread along Rue Verdun for luxury goods, but our favorite destination was Hamra Street. We told Sonja, Missy, and Troy that they could each buy one special item. We would purchase the necessities, like underclothes, pajamas, and so on. Missy bought capri pants and a top, Sonja a special party dress, and Troy persuaded us to buy a toy machine gun and a plastic soldier's helmet, items he saw on the soldiers in Cairo.

Lebanon's population was highly diverse but divided along religious lines rather than ethnic ones. There were Sunni Muslims, Shiite Muslims, Druze, Maronite Christians, Greek Orthodox Christians, Catholic, and Protestant groups. In addition, there were Palestinians displaced during conflicts with Israel, and Armenians, a minority community with its own cultural identity.

This was not a melting pot of religions. It was a fragile state with a delicate sectarian balance. The country divided political power among the major religious groups. The presidency was allocated to Maronite Christians, the prime minister's position to Sunni Muslims, and the parliamentary speaker's role to Shiite Muslims. However, at the time of our visit in 1973, tensions rose due to growing dissatisfaction among Muslim communities about their representation and rights. Additionally, the presence of Palestinian refugees and militias, like the Palestine Liberation Organization (PLO), created further instability. From 1975 to 1990, Lebanon was to be engaged in a civil war.

▲ ▲ ▲

As a group, we numbered eleven people, so we didn't fit into one taxi. Just by chance, our family's personal taxi driver, Ibrahim, a Maronite Christian, became our guide for a later trip we made to Lebanese mountain villages and tourist destinations. Not only were his charges reasonable, but he also wanted us to meet his family. He invited us to lunch at his modest home in a village just above Beirut. His wife and two adult sons were wonderful hosts, and the home-cooked food was delicious.

Ibrahim wanted to take us on an adult-only trip with Bob and Joyce to see the Shatila Refugee Camp for Palestinians on the outskirts of the city. In 1973, Beirut hosted a significant number of Palestinian refugees who had fled their homeland due to the Arab-Israeli conflict in 1965. Shatila became one of the most impoverished and densely populated camps in Lebanon. Ibrahim didn't want us to get out of the car, but he stopped across the street so we could get a good view of it. The camp was overcrowded with makeshift shelters made of corrugated metal and concrete blocks. Necessities such as clean water, toilets, showers, and healthcare were evidently lacking.

"Most people in Beirut don't like the Shatila people," Ibrahim told us, "so they can't find jobs in the city. Some of them have guns and fight among themselves. Sometimes, the ones with guns fight with Lebanese who want to control neighborhoods of Beirut."

This was our first experience with displaced people and their struggles. The Palestinian experience has been marked by displacement, exile, and statelessness. I wouldn't have believed that fifty-two years later, the Palestinian situation would be more dire than ever. On March 24, 2025, Reuters news agency reported more than 50,000 Palestinians had been killed in Gaza with nearly a third of the dead under 18, according to Palestinian health authorities,

▲ ▲ ▲

Our batch of children was immune from political problems. They had discovered the inviting hotel pool overlooking the Mediterranean. Swimming became a daily activity. There was no lifeguard, so we had to be certain that one of the adults was present all the time. Unfortunately, I wasn't a good swimmer, so Floyd was watching over Troy, who was still a beginner but becoming more proficient from his lessons at the Ma'adi Club. Brian counted as an adult now because he was thirteen and had training as a youth lifeguard back in Ohio. The pool was on the same high promontory as the hotel. It had a slide, a diving board, a kiddie pool, and shower fixtures on the side of the pool facing the sea.

I was stretched out on a lounge chair reading a book while Floyd was chatting with Bob beside the pool. Sonja was helping Troy rinse off under the shower before drying off. I heard Sonja scream and saw her trying to hold onto Troy's hand. Evidently, he had stepped onto pieces of soap and slid under the bars that protected the shower from the side of the cliff, which dropped into the sea about twenty feet below. We all rushed to the railing and saw Troy dog paddling to a rock that jutted out from the cliff.

"Hang onto the rock, Troy! We'll get down to you," Floyd shouted.

Floyd and Bob tried to see if they could get around the bars and find a way down to Troy.. One of the German tourists tried to be helpful by telling us he had seen sharks there yesterday. Bob ran into the hotel to get help. Troy wasn't crying or panicking like the rest of us.

It wasn't long until we spotted a man climbing over rocks down below to reach Troy. He had been fishing at a spot on the other side of the cliff when he heard us shouting. He managed to help Troy to get to the other side of the rocks and out of danger. He lifted Troy up to us. With many thanks to the fisherman, we wrapped Troy up in a towel and gave him lots of hugs. Thank God for the swimming lessons from Ibrahim at the Ma'adi Club. Troy's reaction?

"I was just a little scared," he said.

Here we were again in a life-or-death situation. Was it our fault for not being more cautious? Should Floyd and I have been watching Troy more closely? Was it the fault of the hotel for not enclosing the showers? Or our mistake for not checking out their location? Yes, to all of these, but the same question remains: Were we irresponsible for bringing our children to the Middle East? Should we have stayed on a safe campus in the US? We could have protected our children more easily but then, again, accidents and illnesses can happen, even in America. We needed to carefully allow our children to experience life without being overly cautious. I knew from experience what it was like to be the only child of a mother who was fearful of some unknown disaster happening to me. I might drown if I swam. I might get hit by a car if I bicycled in the street. I might break my arm if I climbed a tree. I was trying hard to find a balance in my child-raising attitudes. I realized Floyd and I had a constant responsibility to make wise decisions as we continued our lives in Cairo.

The Beirut experience was a reset button for me. It reminded me that life is precious and not to be wasted on petty concerns. Each day in a new country held the possibility of beauty, love of family, and joy in new experiences. My frustration with aspects of Egyptian culture was minor in comparison. I was beginning to understand the two angry episodes I had before our trip to Beirut. The taxi driver who insisted on overcharging me was an example of the common occurrence of being taken advantage of. It grew out of the widespread poverty and the necessity to just get by another day. I was an easy target as an American. My money could make life easier for the family of the taxi driver, the Mousky salesman, or even Salim. However, the sexual perversion of the cyclist exposing himself was more difficult to fathom. I knew that Islam didn't condone such behavior, but social rules around interactions between men and women were very strict and led to what ex-patriate women called "sex-starved men" who exhibited unhealthy behavior toward women. Unfortunately, Egyptian society tolerated these actions.

Our spring vacation came to an end. We packed our bags with our cherished purchases. Troy's plastic machine gun wouldn't fit into his suitcase, so we allowed him to carry it on in a shopping bag. Not a wise decision. As we went through a baggage check before boarding, an official told him he could not have the toy on the passenger side of the airplane because it looked too real. They would put it inside the cockpit, and he could retrieve it when we reached our destination. How naïve we were to even let him have the gun! It might have been permissible in the US but not in Lebanon or Egypt, two countries that would be engaged in their own conflicts soon.

Five Piastres

Five piastres buy
Pearls of jasmine laced on string
a spicy mystery.

Hoopoe

Proud Hopoe with your
striped hood, did you strut so
for King Solomon?

14

Home Leave

SUMMER QUICKLY APPROACHED, with a plethora of farewell parties, school programs, and vacation preparations. Sonja and Missy said farewell to friends moving abroad while appreciating those staying in Cairo. Troy's best friends, Justin and Paul, would still be buddies in the preschool we had organized two years ago.

We extended our contract with the university by two years, allowing us to visit Europe before returning to Colorado. AUC paid for our airfare from Cairo to Colorado and back. And, best of all, we could apply the airfare home to any side trips we might take on the way. When we returned to Cairo, however, we would join the annual AUC flight with new hires and continuing faculty.

Our plans for June included visits to London, Denmark, and Switzerland. I was most excited by the prospect of meeting my Danish relatives. My Grandfather Grondahl had immigrated to the US in the 1880s. My mom cherished this heritage, learned Danish, and wrote letters to her relatives in the Danish peninsula of Jylland from the time she was a child until she died. Several years ago, she had won a trip to Denmark in a writing contest run by the Peter Heering Company. She and my dad took the trip of a lifetime to meet all the Grondahl relatives in person. Now, it was my turn.

When we returned to Colorado after our four weeks abroad, we would stay with Floyd's parents in Littleton, visit with my mom and dad in Denver, see my grandmother in Longmont, and meet many of our friends in Fort Collins. Seeing us alive and well would reassure our parents that we might survive another two years in Cairo. Floyd was still very thin and gaunt from his bout of cholera, so that was a worry. I could predict they would try to talk us out of returning to Egypt.

Preparations for this trip involved some other apprehensions about leaving behind the villa and the kids' beloved pets: Snoopy, Patches, and Richard. The university planned to paint and do some repairs to the house while we were away, but Salim would still be there to oversee our possessions and to feed the animals—we hoped. I know he thought we were crazy Americans who loved animals more than people. Not true. We loved people a tad more than animals, but it was easier to help animals.

▲ ▲ ▲

Our European trip swept us into another world: exploring sophisticated cities, eating unique foods, riding double-decker buses, touching the weird statues at Madame Tussaud's Wax Museum, seeing *Jesus Christ SuperStar* in a small London theater, thrilling on the rides in Tivoli Gardens, sleeping in beds with goose down pillows and comforters, meeting interesting and accomplished Scandinavian relatives, swimming in the Baltic Sea with my nude great uncle, riding a funicular up a mountain in the Swiss Alps, and staying in a small Christian abolitionist hotel in a Swiss village next to a zoo.

Our visit to my Danish relatives prepared us for the current political scene in the US. When the conversation turned to American politics and President Richard Nixon, they laughed and said, "What's the big deal? European leaders are involved in scandals like this all the time."

They were talking about the Watergate Scandal. The breaking news was the discovery that Nixon's re-election campaign members had broken into and planted listening devices in the Democratic National Committee headquarters at the Watergate office building in Washington, DC. We followed this news story and others during our vacation. We were eager for accurate information about American politics and how it might affect Egypt.

We arrived at Stapleton International Airport in Denver exhausted but happy. Our parents welcomed us with tears, open arms, and shock about Floyd's weight loss. Our close friends, Bill and Lucy Brenner, in Fort Collins, didn't even recognize Floyd when we knocked on their door. He was "skinny and pale." I encouraged Floyd to have a physical exam while we were here. He had a check-up with his parents' internal medicine doctor, who prescribed an antibiotic for an infection that may have caused a peptic ulcer, and vitamins to build up his resistance.

▲ ▲ ▲

The time in Denver gave us the chance to clarify our experiences in Egypt from the perspective of our past lives in the US. We had only been away for two years, but so much had changed. My parents looked good and had developed a closer relationship rather than focusing on me, their only child. They had just moved to a down-town Volunteers of America senior apartment. My dad, who was now just sixty-three, had retired early from his position as a radio engineer at KOA radio and TV, when he lost most of his retirement funds in the sale of the station from Bob Hope Associates to Metro Television. He was disgusted with management and decided it was time to retire.

Floyd's dad had retired from the Colorado Cooperative Extension Service as an Arapahoe County 4-H agent in 1971, just before we left for Cairo. His parents had purchased an old ranch in the Black Forest that kept them continually occupied with repairs, livestock, and more. They were involved in the lives of their other grandchildren and their problems and achievements. Their Denver sons, Forrest and Gene, were active in their daily experiences and concerns.

Other people now occupied the Fort Collins houses we had owned when our children were born. Our friends and relatives were initially interested in our Cairo experiences but soon changed the conversations to what was happening in their lives. Basically, no one was as interested in hearing about our adventures as we were about sharing them. This was not a rejection of our stories and achievements but simply a reflection of the fact that once they had heard the highlights, they felt like they'd heard everything. Was this the Thomas Wolfe "You Can't Go Home Again" experience or just a normal part of being surprised or shocked at how different life was in the States? At first, we felt that everything in the US had changed. As the summer progressed and we tried to balance our lives in two countries, we made a discovery. We were the ones who had changed.

Sonja, Missy, and Troy enjoyed watching American TV, experiencing Grandad's ranch in the Black Forest, and visiting the shopping centers. As usual, shopping for items we couldn't buy in Cairo occupied some of our time. We bought a metal trunk to hold our purchases of food, school clothes, and items we could no longer find in Cairo shops. AUC would allow this rather heavy trunk as part of our luggage on the return trip. Interestingly, the kids missed parts of their daily lives at "home" in Cairo. While stroking the nose of one of Grandad's horses, Missy thought about her favorite Ma'adi Club horse, Mabruk, and rides at the pyramids with friends on the weekend. Sonja wrote a letter to her Swedish friend, Cecelia, to tell her about our trip to Denmark. Troy wished to have his Big Wheels to ride around the small concrete space at Grandma Shoemaker's house.

What was happening in US politics intrigued us. Now, we could eagerly consume news about the escalating tensions in Cairo and its allies from the perspective of the side that supported Israel. Corruption had taken over the front pages of American newspapers and TV screens. President Richard Nixon was at the end of his first term in office when we left for Cairo in 1971. In June 1973, while we traveled in Europe, the Watergate Scandal burst onto the scene. It began with the arrest of five burglars at the Democratic National Committee headquarters. The burglars were connected to Nixon's reelection campaign and were caught wiretapping phones and stealing documents. Although Floyd's parents weren't as involved in politics, they joined us to watch the Senate Watergate Committee televised hearings investigating the Watergate scandal. These hearings revealed crucial information about the involvement of high-ranking officials in the Nixon administration in covering up the break-in and other illegal activities. Calls for his impeachment had begun in earnest.

Would this affect the US attitude toward Egypt and their potential war against Israel? President Nixon and his national security advisor, Henry Kissinger, were extremely cautious about engaging with Egypt despite President Sadat's efforts to open diplomatic channels. President Sadat had expelled Soviet advisors the previous year in an effort to facilitate US assistance in resolving the Arab-Israeli conflict. He had offered a proposal for peace between the two countries, contingent on Israeli withdrawal from territories occupied in 1967. However, the US had remained skeptical of Sadat's intentions and did not act on his proposal, believing that Egypt would not attack Israel because it did not have the military strength to win a war. Previous political concerns played a part in the American attitude. Nixon and Kissinger did not want to put potential strains on US-Israeli relations before the 1972 presidential elections. They also were cautious about initiating any American diplomatic efforts until after Israel's elections in October.

American politics was also in the foreground when the women's liberation movement in the US reached its peak while we were overseas. I had relished Betty Friedan's *Feminine Mystique* in the '60s and was fascinated by what had happened. Recently, American women had begun advocating for gender equality in education, employment, and legal rights. They had started to question traditional roles as homemakers and looked for greater independence. More women pursued higher education during this period, with a focus on developing a career rather than only preparing for marriage. Society's expectations for women were shifting. I applauded the advances women engaged in and realized that my life reflected some of these changes. I was not a traditional stay-at-home wife, but I had prioritized my husband's aspirations in choosing to teach rather than pursuing a full-time journalism career. I was a mother of three children. I had a master's degree. And now I had relative independence in Cairo to rediscover my writing aspirations.

▲ ▲ ▲

The overseas news that worried our parents and made us anxious was set aside, so we could enjoy the last few weeks with our extended family. We said our goodbyes to everyone in late August. Despite the comfort of family life, we all wanted to return to Cairo, knowing we would aim for Colorado after another two years at AUC.

It was *deja vu* to leave from New York on a chartered plane to Cairo. Old faculty members relaxed and visited, and newly hired professors and their families were a bit apprehensive but excited and eager to ask questions from the older and wiser group. When we finally landed in Cairo, we couldn't wait to hurry home to see if our pets were OK. Mohamed, our new AUC expediter, told us that work on our villa wasn't quite finished, so we would need to stay in another villa temporarily. What a disappointment! As soon as our bags were unloaded at the replacement villa, we walked over to Road 19, Number 48. Salim and Ayoub cheerfully met us in the garden, where Troy found his Big Wheels. Salim was happy to see us and shook hands all around. After thanking him for his care of the villa, we had questions.

"Is Snoopy still here in the garden?" I asked.

"Where are the cats?" Missy chimed in.

Salim nodded affirmatively. "Everything OK. Salim take good care."

While the kids looked for the cats, I went around the garden looking for Snoopy. I found her by the garage. She immediately ran to me, nudged my hand for a stroke, and sat down beside me. I could see that her coat was free of mange, but she had a few ticks attached to her belly. She appeared to be pregnant. *Oh, my,* I thought, *what will we do with puppies?*

We found Patches and Richard on the tiny, unused balcony outside our bedroom. They had crawled up the trellis to find a cool spot on an old wicker chair. They were skinny and hungry—but alive.

It was two weeks before we got to move back into the villa. Everything was newly painted, waxed, and washed. As I was unpacking our bags in the bedroom, I looked into the tiny built-in cupboard next to the closet. I had put my jewelry box underneath some belts and scarves. The box contained inexpensive costume jewelry plus one small diamond ring gifted to me in a competition I had won. I didn't particularly like the ring and had never worn it, instead leaving it in the box. When I looked through the jewelry, I discovered that this ring was the only item missing. I could have just said "*Ma'alesh*" and considered it a contribution to one of the many university workmen in the house while we were away, but I thought I should report the loss to the university housing office. I mentioned it to Salim when he asked me if everything in the villa was good.

When I told him about the ring, he panicked.

"No, no, Madame. Salim no take ring. Bad to tell university."

I explained that I didn't think he had taken the ring, but I thought the university housing office should know that it was missing.

"University tell police, and police take Salim. Police ..." He made a fist and punched at the air to indicate hitting.

I should have known that police arrests often lead to beatings to extract confessions, regardless of guilt. Tears began running down Salim's plump cheeks. He wiped them away with his apron.

"No problem, Salim. *Ma'alesh.* I won't tell the university. Don't worry."

I patted his shoulder. He offered many *shukrans* and hurried back to the kitchen.

We settled into the villa just in time for school to begin. Floyd was already inundated with work on a new semester at AUC. Fewer Americans enrolled in classes at the university this fall, but there were new students from Nigeria, Congo, Syria, and Tunisia. Apprehension about Egypt and Israel had dampened American students' enthusiasm.

On our second night back in the refurbished villa, an air raid siren splitting the air from the nearby military building shocked us out of bed. The electricity in our suburb had been cut off earlier in the evening, which was not unusual, but we had never experienced an air raid drill. The protocol was to take shelter, turn the lights out, and close the shutters until the all-clear sounded. Friends who had been here all summer told us that the drills happened once or twice a week. About thirty minutes later, a muted siren indicated all clear.

Welcome back!

Air Alert, October 6, 1973

The crows
are the first to know,
exploding
from pine-tree heights,
feathered
fragments of shrapnel
shrieking
caws of alarm.

Dull thuds
of artillery
play bass
to the crows' raw cry,
then dust
sifts into silent specks
cut clean
by the siren moan.

15

Ramadan War

TROY AND PAUL hunted for frogs in the garden while I cleaned off the sandy grime from my bicycle. I saw Salim wheeling his bicycle toward our gate. Early this morning, he had gone to Saad's butcher shop in Old Ma'adi determined to buy some chicken. All meats, sugar, and tea were in short supply because feeding the army came first. Salim was grumbling when he left, complaining about the long lines shoppers had to stand in just to get up to the window where they placed their orders.

He was having trouble opening the gate while he held onto the bike. When I went to help him, I noticed his right hand was wrapped in a bloody rag.

"*Eh, da,* Salim? What happened? Are you okay?"

"Not OK, Madame. Butcher very bad. I wait and wait long time. Then Saad say, 'One chicken left. You pay four pounds.' *Abadan!* I pay four pounds."

With his left hand, Salim pointed and shook his index finger and then clamped his teeth together several times. Evidently, the butcher had leaned forward and bitten the tip of Salim's finger. I told him to go inside and I would clean his finger and put a bandage on it. It was true. Saad, the butcher, had bitten off the very tip of the offending finger.

The event fascinated Troy and Paul, and they watched while I got out the first aid kit and cleaned and bandaged the finger. I wasn't looking forward to a dinner cooked with his bandaged hand, so I told Salim to take the day off and go home.

"*Shukran, shukran,* Madame. Salim go. *Bukra insha' Allah.*"

God willing, he'd be back tomorrow.

I fixed the boys a snack of grapes from the garden, some cookies, and juice. I sat with them on the back patio while they ate.

Amel, the Ferrar's nanny, found us there when she came to walk Paul home. She was wearing a knee-length white dress and a blue cardigan sweater. Her hair was pulled back in a ponytail held by a blue barrette, and she was wearing pink lipstick. She could easily have been mistaken for an American teenager. Her teenage life, however, had been filled with adult responsibilities and tragedy.

Amel and I had become well-acquainted through her job with our friends Joyce and Bob and their kids. She spoke much better English than Salim, so we had talked at length on her visits to our house. This gave me the opportunity to hear the story of a woman who was among the thousands of village people who had migrated to Cairo for a better life. I wanted to learn about her life, and she wanted to share it.

Amel had come from a village in the Fayoum, about seventy miles from Cairo. She had been promised in marriage at thirteen to Amr, an eighteen-year-old. They were married a year later and moved to Cairo, where Amr began studying engineering at a technical school and working in a factory. The young couple lived in a two-room apartment in Shoubra with Amr's aunt and uncle. They were soon joined in the same apartment by Amr's mother when his father died.

"Baby come fast," Amel said, "*ma'sha'allah!,*" thanks be to God!

She had become pregnant after six months of marriage. Events rushed on precipitously. Her new husband was drafted into the army to fight in the 1967 Arab-Israeli War. After basic training, he was transported to active duty in the Sinai Peninsula. This was the Six-Day War that precipitated the current preparations for war with Israel. Their son, Saeed, was born while he was fighting in the losing battle with Israel. It wasn't until Saeed was six months old that Amr got home leave.

"Amr, Amel, and Saeed, a good family then," she nodded and smiled in remembrance. "Amr so happy to have a son! I happy to have Amr here."

Home leave meant the chance for them to become reacquainted and practice being a real family. It also meant another pregnancy for Amel. Once Amr had returned to service, her mother-in-law would not allow pregnant Amel to take Saeed outside the apartment.

"Mother-in-law love Saeed but not like Amel. I work hard for her, but no love," she said.

Troy and Paul had finished their sandwiches and a bunch of grapes from the garden. It was time for Amel to hurry home to help Joyce with preparations for dinner. She stood up and paused for a minute to reach into her pocket. She pulled out a tattered envelope to show me.

It was the only letter she had ever received. I couldn't read the Arabic, but I could see it had a picture of the Egyptian flag and several official stamps. It was the official government notification of Amr's death in fighting near the Sinai border. Amr was just one of an estimated ten to fifteen thousand Egyptian soldiers and several hundred to several thousand Palestinian civilians killed in the Six-Day War.

"Amr gone. Amr dead, *ma'shallah*." It was God's will. Four months later, baby Dina was born.

Her voice quavered. She pointed to a black-rimmed box at the end of the letter.

"*Talata ganee, kulli sahr.*" Three pounds widow's allowance, about $5 each month.

I couldn't fathom this. Here she was face-to-face with a life that involved two babies, a widowed mother-in-law and a monthly rent that equaled her three-pound widow's allowance. I folded up the letter and returned it to her.

"I'm so sorry, Amel."

All I could manage was to give her a hug, pack up Paul's toys to take home, and say goodbye until the next visit.

▲ ▲ ▲

The 1973–74 school year had just begun. Troy had turned five in December, so he qualified for the half-day CAC kindergarten. He was excited about going to the same school as his sisters. Sonja and Missy's classes were a bit smaller than the fifteen to twenty students usually enrolled, probably because of the war scare. Sonja was back with Madame Laurella and her classes *en pointe* with new toe shoes from the States. She continued to raid the well-stocked CAC library and focused on Greek mythology and books by Alexander Dumas.

Missy, with English riding lessons under her belt, enjoyed horse-back riding at the pyramids on weekends with a classmate and her family. She and Elinore still spent time at the Ma'adi Club eating sandwiches in the garden and playing detective. The Egyptian kids who worked in the kitchen occasionally teased them, and Elinore and Missy had fun returning the insults. Their favorite rejoinder was "*yikrib beitak!*" May your house be destroyed! This was sometimes preceded by "*Ya gamusa!*" Hey, water buffalo!

▲ ▲ ▲

It was September 28. The beginning of Ramadan was fast approaching. The atmosphere was not as festive as it had been our first two years, but Muslims still anticipated the holy month as a way of relieving the tensions of daily life. The sense of dedication and spirituality was obvious. People cleaned and decorated their houses and tried to buy scarce food items and ingredients needed for preparing special meals, which usually included dates, lentils, rice, meats, and fruits, most of which were missing from the marketplace. More time was spent at the mosque and reading the Qur'an.

I remembered Troy sharing *iftar,* the meal to break the fast at sunset, with the cooks at the apartment house during our first

Ramadan here. He particularly loved the dates that initiated the end of the day's fasting from water and food. Salim sometimes made *fattah* for our family. It was a popular holiday dish made with rice, bread, meat and a garlic-tomato sauce. My favorite was *kunafa*, a sweet dessert made with thin noodle-like pastry soaked in sugar syrup and filled with cheese or nuts. It was another Ramadan dessert that required sugar, which was now almost impossible to find, except on the black market.

Floyd and Bob made daily trips to the university. Bob still wanted to immerse himself in the culture by riding in second-class. Bad luck seemed to pursue him. On the first day back in the office, the duo was squeezed in the back of a train car behind a woman with a chicken crate on her head and her three small children in grimy *galabiyas*. With no room for briefcases in their arms, Bob and Floyd placed them on the floor between their legs, as usual. At the Tahrir Square stop, they quickly grabbed the briefcases before being pushed out the doors and onto the platform. Bob stopped to check his briefcase. It was covered with the feces from a bare bottom. One of the little boys had sat on the end of Bob's briefcase. Underwear was a luxury for the poor children who rode in second-class cars.

During Ramadan, AUC would begin a limited class schedule of more morning classes and shorter hours. They also alerted the faculty and staff of measures to ensure the safety of staff and students in response to a possible outbreak of war after Ramadan. The university would close its doors and advise all non-Egyptian students and non-essential staff to evacuate the country. Essential personnel, including faculty and administrative staff, were required to remain on campus to maintain critical university functions. We didn't know of any students or staff members who left. War seemed like a distant threat, both timewise and also miles away.

▲ ▲ ▲

Ramadan began and life went on as usual for our family, with school, fun, and movies at the Ma'adi Club, ballet lessons from non-fasting Catholic Madame Laurella, and the beginning of my special journalism class for the feisty Yugoslavians at CAC. Military personnel fasted, but helicopters kept flying in convoys throughout the day, and Army trucks rumbled through the streets. We could hear patriotic music on Salim's radio in the kitchen. With the threat of potential air raids, citizens and foreign residents were again instructed to participate in drills to prepare for possible attacks. Public buildings, schools, and residential areas had designated shelters where people would gather during these drills or actual attacks.

Just a week into Ramadan, at one p.m. on Thursday, October 6, the air alert siren blasted away for fifteen minutes, stopped, and sounded again. People on the streets shook their heads in disbelief. Not during Ramadan! During the second alarm, people took it seriously and hurried to find a place to take shelter. Sonja and Missy had just returned to their afternoon classes after lunch. Teachers made sure everyone was inside. They calmed the students and continued with classes.

Word soon spread. Egyptian and Syrian forces had launched a surprise attack on Israeli positions in the Sinai Peninsula and the Golan Heights. It was Yom Kippur, the Day of Atonement, the holiest day in the Jewish calendar. Many Israeli soldiers were away from their posts, observing the day with their families. No one on either side of the conflict could believe that war would be initiated during Ramadan and on Yom Kippur. This was Sadat's daring plan to attack Israel. Even if it was unsuccessful, he hoped that it might convince Israelis that peace with Egypt was necessary. It was also necessary for Sadat, as the leader of an economically troubled nation that could not afford to continue its crusade against Israel. Peace and recovery of the Sinai could achieve the stability Egypt needed to continue the country's development.

The war's sudden outbreak caused panic for many in the ex-patriot community and for tourists throughout Egypt. The proximity of the war increased tensions and safety concerns for foreign nationals. Evacuations were part of broader efforts by many foreign governments and companies to ensure the safety and well-being of their citizens. Evacuations of friends and neighbors took place around us. AMOCO had approximately one thousand employees working in Egypt. Many of our friends in Ma'adi were among these families. As I wrote about the evacuations, I contacted my friend Nancy Cronen, who was married to an AMOCO executive. We had maintained contact for fifty years. I asked her about her memories of that time. She told me that AMOCO decided to leave families in Egypt rather than temporarily evacuate them, as they did during the 1967 War with Israel. At that time, husbands could stay in Egypt and would receive a one-thousand-dollar bonus. During that war, Nancy's husband stayed, and the family went on to Athens until it was safe to return.

▲ ▲ ▲

"I remember I had come back from the Ma'adi Club tennis court," Nancy said. "My cook Abdul said something to the effect 'they're at it again.' At first, I thought he was talking about my two boys, but he was whispering. I finally caught on to what he meant: the beginning of the war. The very next day, some Egyptian men came around and painted all the windows blue. Also, the Ma'adi Club was closed, and there were no more movies. We received cards for gas, but we never ran out because we had nowhere to go. Our blue VW also had a reserve tank. For extra security, we paid some local Egyptians to guard the car."

Nancy continued, "One evening, we had to drive to Cairo to visit the AMOCO doctor. When we couldn't start our car, we realized that someone had stolen a part. We got some men to help push it, but it kept stopping down the road. We finally got to the Corniche. When it stopped again, local Egyptians pushed it without being asked. We also had our horn stolen but got it replaced by the owner of the Ma'adi Bike Shop."

▲ ▲ ▲

Nancy's account of the war from an oil company family's view contrasts with that of AUC families. In both situations, however, danger did not seem imminent enough to send Americans out of the country.

We experienced a strong support system from AUC and our Egyptian colleagues and friends. The university closed its doors for classes and advised all non-Egyptian students and staff to leave the country if possible. Essential personnel, including faculty and administrative staff, were required to offer the remaining students lectures, workshops, and other educational activities to keep them engaged and motivated. They provided emotional support and counseling to those who struggled with the stress and trauma of the war. The university also offered support to diplomats, journalists, and other foreign nationals whose jobs required them to stay in Egypt or who were unable to leave because of travel restrictions and the closure of the Cairo International Airport. The campus became a haven for the international community.

Students who remained in apartments near the campus faced community shortages of food, water, and other essential supplies. Additionally, the threat of violence and the uncertainty of the war created a tense and stressful atmosphere on campus. We opened our doors to Ewart Skinner, a student from Trinidad-Tobago who had stayed with us when he first came to AUC. Troy welcomed him to the second bed in his room in hopes of engaging him in racing Matchbox cars. Ewart brought a transistor radio that could access Voice of Israel, the BBC, and, of course, Cairo Radio. This allowed us three different perspectives on the daily news from the Sinai and the Golan Heights.

The university was in a difficult position with its ties to the US and its reliance on Egypt for its very existence.

▲ ▲ ▲

In the AUC *The Caravan* newspaper dated October 17:

AUC cables Sadat, Nixon, "In its Saturday, October 13 meeting the program committee sent a telegram of support on behalf of the faculty and staff of AUC to President Anwar el-Sadat. The committee also sent another cable to President Richard Nixon, asking the US government to follow an even-handed policy on the Middle East conflict.

The cable was signed by non-Egyptian members of the faculty.

What happened to the tourists in Egypt? It was reported later that as many as 450 people, under the guidance of the U.S. Embassy in Cyprus, were rounded up throughout Egypt, taken to Cairo hotels, and then transported in buses and cars over the desert to Alexandria. From there, after waiting for days for a ship, they sailed to Athens and then took flights home to the US. I pictured our family packing a few bags, saying goodbye to friends and pets, and traveling across the desert with a bunch of complaining tourists. I was thankful that we got to stay in the safety of our home in Ma'adi, where our colleagues and all the Egyptians we knew were concerned about and protective of us.

The evacuations affected CAC's population. Students remaining in Ma'adi were scheduled to meet at their teachers' homes once a week to get instruction and assignments to complete at home. Sonja and Missy read, did homework, and still went to the Ma'adi Club for recreation.

The kids basically went on with their regular lives. Troy played at the Ferrar's house nearby or here at home in the garden. Sonja and Missy did their homework and walked over to the club to sit in the garden and visit with friends. All regular sports areas at the club were open, but no swimming or riding lessons were scheduled. It was an exciting time for them with a bit of fear mixed in. We still had alarms at dusk to remind us of blackouts. We always shuttered our windows and kept our minds attuned to any sounds of war. The fighting was about one hundred and seventy miles away and not on Egyptian soil. We couldn't hear any gunfire, bombs, or artillery.

During blackouts, Floyd, Ewart, and I huddled together in candle-light at the end of our dining room table with our ears attuned to the radio reports. Salim also listened in the kitchen to Egyptian news in Arabic and would pop around the corner to flash the victory sign. Radio Israel announced huge victories just as Egyptian radio did. We soon discovered that the only reliable source of impartial news was the BBC.

The pomp and circumstance of victory filled the first few broadcasts on Egyptian radio. Arab forces were making significant gains. However, when we checked with Israel's broadcasts, we heard that they had quickly mobilized forces in a huge counter-offensive that pushed back the Arab forces. As the days progressed, so did the Israeli counter-offensive.

Just a few days into the war, we had a scare. Missy and Elinore had gone to the Ma'adi Club to "hang out," as they said, with friends in the garden. The rest of us were at home in the villa. An air raid siren sounded for ten minutes, stopped, and sounded again. Missy and Elinore had just started toward home. They decided it was too far to take shelter at home, so they ran up to one of the villas near the club and knocked on the door. A very kind Egyptian lady invited them in until the all-clear sounded. She also offered them tea and biscuits. We discovered in listening to the BBC later that the alarm sounded because Israel had pushed back the Arab forces and had crossed the Suez Canal into Egypt in addition to advancing on to Damascus, Syria.

▲ ▲ ▲

Before we knew it, the Ramadan (or Yom Kippur) War was over. It ended on the nineteenth day, October 25, 1973, when a ceasefire was brokered by the United Nations before either side could declare victory. However, it was considered a strategic victory for Egypt and Syria as they were able to restore some of their lost pride after previous defeats against Israel. There were no declared victors because both sides were supported by powerful international backers, the US for Israel and the Soviet Union for Egypt and Syria. Neither side had gained a decisive advantage. The ceasefire lines largely reflected the pre-war borders between Israel and its neighbors.

On a positive note, Sadat had used his initial success during the war to seek peace and, as we would see in the next two years, to sign disengagement agreements with Israel that provided for the return of portions of the Sinai Peninsula to Egypt. The negative aspect was the huge loss of life that devastated thousands of families.

Canal Crossing

What price for boys who die like flies?
Piastres, pounds, allotments paid
three guinea a month for each demise
to give the widow paltry aid.

The cost of lumber isn't cheap,
but a bridge of bodies flung across
the sanguine Suez will not reap
its weight in dollars or in dross.

What price for boys who die like flies?
Only the cost of mortar shells,
bare wooden coffins built to size,
the recitation of farewells.

Ceasefire
October 22, 1973

She balances on the foxhole's brim,
lick, licking a paw to preen her ears
a calico sponge that drinks the sun
leaving just a drop to light the gray
muzzle of the corporal's machine gun.

16

Aftermath

JUST TWO DAYS after the ceasefire, the feast of *Eid al-Fitr* began. This year, there were no fireworks or street performers. Instead, there was a scarcity of eggs, sugar, coffee, tea, and *butagaz* to cook the special *Eid* food, and there was not enough money for the average Egyptian to buy new clothes. The traditional celebrations were influenced by a complex mix of pride in military efforts against Israel and a somber recognition of losses during the war. Eight to ten thousand Egyptian soldiers had been killed, and thousands of families were missing loved ones. On the other side of the war, twenty-five hundred to three thousand Israeli soldiers were dead. The atmosphere was one where traditional family celebrations coexisted with mourning for the lost. Then, too, there was an undercurrent of national pride. Compared to our previous experiences with *Eid al-Fitr* holidays, this year was quiet and subdued. Salim, Semeha, and Ayoub showed relief to be finished with fasting and expressed gratitude for the extra money we offered to them for their family celebrations.

▲ ▲ ▲

At the top of our immediate concerns was a call home to our parents to let them know we were alive and well. We knew how worried they would be as they read the newspapers and watched American television. We could not make calls during the war. Even making them after the war required special permission and an appointment for the call. The calls had to be monitored by the government. We waited five days for our appointment. After several attempts, we got through to my mom and dad and asked them to call Floyd's parents. Although the connection wasn't very clear, I could tell my mother was crying. She told me she had been sick just waiting for a message. They had been relying on Denver newspapers for reports of the war and pictured bombs falling on our villa and killing us all. No matter how much we reassured them of our safety, they urged us to return to the States.

A huge part of their worry was the fact our communication with them was basically limited to letters and, recently, of course, delivered intermittently. If our US and international families were involved in the same situation today, we would be able to communicate through a combination of technologies: smartphones and messaging apps, the internet, Zoom, Google, Skype, emails, satellite phones, and more.

▲ ▲ ▲

With the end of the war, the Cairo Airport opened, and passengers departed and arrived. Ewart stayed with us for another week and then returned to his apartment near the university. He hoped to take a quick trip home to Trinidad before the January semester began. AUC had strengthened its ties with the Egyptian government and other institutions during the war. It was making plans to expand its academic programs and research initiatives focusing on issues related to peace, security, and development, becoming a key partner in the country's efforts to modernize and reform its education system. Floyd's program in mass communication became even more important. This validated our decision to commit to another two years in Cairo.

Sonja, Missy, and Troy happily had more freedom now and could return to school. The Ramadan War signaled the thawing of

Egyptian-US relations and the return of American families to Egypt in much larger numbers than before. In the past months, CAC had been receiving advance enrollments from students whose families would be transferred to Cairo as a number of US and other foreign companies began working in Egypt. During the remaining time we were there, total enrollment increased from 343 to 1293 students. The percentage of American students grew from forty-four to sixty-three percent. Egyptian students were able to enroll and their enrollment, starting from zero, grew by seven percent, according to the school's archives.

▲ ▲ ▲

Back home at the villa, we had another "rebirth." Troy was busy harassing Ayoub in the garden by accidentally running his Big Wheels into the huge pots of geraniums. Instead of scolding him, Ayoub led him to some wooden crates next to the garage.

"Look! See?" he directed. "*Kalb bebe.*"

Snoopy had given birth to six puppies. The dog I had cured of mange, protected against rabies, and brought back to health now had six brown and white puppies. It was hard enough to feed Snoopy and the cats. Pet food was unavailable, so Salim saved scraps and boiled chicken bones to feed Snoopy and the house cats, who also hunted for mice in the garden for additional food. I was already ashamed to have my poor Egyptian cook preparing food for pets when he was having trouble feeding his own family.

The cats we had adopted had been spayed and neutered by the neighborhood veterinarian, Dr. Saleh, an Egyptian trained in vet medicine in England. He was also the vet for the Ma'adi Club horses. However, I had neglected to spay Snoopy. It seemed too difficult to take her from the garden to the clinic. Although I knew we couldn't keep the puppies for the long term, I had Dr. Saleh give them rabies and distemper vaccinations and spay their mother. I knew he would euthanize the pups if I asked him to, but I just didn't have the heart to do that. The children would never forgive me if I did. My Turkish neighbor told me about the British Royal Society for the Prevention of Cruelty to Animals (RSPCA). They would pick up the pups and take them to a no-kill shelter, where they would hopefully be adopted. I explained to the kids that we would keep them until they were old enough to be adopted.

As the pups grew, their tiny yips graduated to louder barks, and the neighbors complained. It was time to call the RSPCA. The lady I spoke to reassured me that they would be well-cared for and placed with families living more permanently in Cairo.

On the day the RSPCA was to come, I was bicycling home from the Harrison's villa with Troy in the seat on the back. About half a block away, I saw a police truck outside the villa with a man yanking one of the puppies up into the truck by a noose tied around its neck. This couldn't be the RSPCA! With a feeling of panic, I turned the corner and went down another street. Luckily, Troy hadn't seen the truck. I just couldn't deal with using my Arabic as an American woman to face the men in the animal control truck, so I ignored what I had seen and turned onto an alternate road to our villa. I was ashamed of not being brave enough to confront the men. This was not the way I wanted to deal with the problem of the puppies barking.

When Troy and I came back to our gate, the dogs were gone, and the irate Turkish neighbor called me over to her driveway.

"You sent your dogs off to be shot. What did you think you were doing?"

Evidently, someone had called the animal control police, and they came before the no-kill shelter arrived. As an animal lover, what had I done? I was crying. Troy was crying.

"I want my puppies back, Mommy."

In this case, I was offered a second chance. I would take a taxi to the other side of Cairo to retrieve the dogs. It took more than an hour to find a taxi driver, whose cab was dilapidated enough he didn't mind putting dogs into the trunk. Troy had to be my accomplice in this act of penance because no one was home to watch him. When we reached the rambling mudbrick building near the Muqattam Hills, I told the taxi driver I would pay him baksheesh kitir if he would wait and take us back to Ma'adi. I wasn't sure what we would do if the driver took off.

When we got out of the taxi, a guard in a rumpled khaki uniform took me to a police captain who spoke English. He laughed at me, an *Amrikaniyya* who loved dogs, but he was won over by Troy, who firmly told him, "I want my dogs!"

He took us to a round enclosure with blood-splattered walls. Our pups were near a low door.

"Madame, go! Get your dogs," the smirking captain said. He gave us some frayed pieces of rope.

Troy and I stepped into the foul-smelling pit. The dogs came to us immediately. We managed to carry or lead them out with ropes tied around their necks into the trunk of the taxi and home to our villa. With the help of the Turkish neighbor, we got them to the RSPCA shelter a few days later.

▲ ▲ ▲

Soon after this event, the university told us Salim was no longer a university cook. I was not given a reason for his removal from the approved list. I knew that he was still putting some money into his own pocket when he padded the grocery costs, but it was difficult for me to check each purchase against the cash I gave him. I had allowed this. Had he actually taken my ring and sold it? Had something happened during our time on home leave? No answers were available. I had stated a year before that I was learning to handle servants firmly. That was not true. Instead, I had developed a *ma'alesh* attitude. Salim's misdeeds were not that important. I was willing to overlook missing *piastres* and unwanted jewelry. Salim needed it more than we did. He was certainly not the best cook and house cleaner, but he was kind and loving. He was also my essential informant on Egyptian attitudes, language, and culture. We would miss him.

We were told that a "more appropriate servant" would be available for us in a few weeks. Meanwhile, we had Kamal, a thirty-five-year-old born in Cairo. Kamal never smiled. He looked sad all the time. I tried to find out why he seemed so unhappy. I asked about his family and children. He told me he loved his wife but had to divorce her and marry a woman his father had chosen.

"My wife, she only give me girls, no boys."

Unfortunately, they had three daughters but no sons in a culture that prized male heirs. His father told him to find a woman who would produce the necessary boys. I sympathized with him and even tried to tell him that it wasn't the wife's fault but soon realized that knowledge wouldn't ease the problem.

After Kamal, Soliman joined us as our newest and most impressive cook. He was fifty-five years old, slim and wiry, with graying hair. His heritage was Bedouin, a nomadic desert tribe. When he came to the city as a young man, his first job was with a British family. Over the years, he had been employed with many British, American, and German families. On his first day at the villa, he asked what kinds of food we liked, jotted them down with a pad and pencil, and said, "Yes, yes, that's good."

I realized that our former cook, Salim, likely could not read or write Arabic well, if at all. Soliman had additional talents. He was a marriage broker, arranging marriages between compatible men and women for a fee. Semeha immediately became his client, hoping he could find her a husband who could overlook her protruding front teeth. Salim performed more services than bringing suitable couples together. He was a clearing house for local tradesmen, folk healers, antiquities sellers, seamstresses, magicians who performed at parties, and even masseuses.

One evening, Salim was serving dinner when he noticed Floyd moving his shoulders back and forth against the dining chair and expressing pain.

"Dr. Floyd hurts?"

"A little bit. I strained my back carrying a trunk in the airport," Floyd said.

"You need Badreya," Salim suggested.

"What's a *badreya*?" I asked.

Salim smiled. "Badreya is a lady. Lady who works on shoulders, backs. She comes to the house. Would you like Salim to get her?"

Floyd thought it was worth trying Badreya, who must be a masseuse. Maybe he could get some relief for his aching back.

Two days later, a five-foot weightlifter of a lady visited Salim at the kitchen door. Salim brought her into the living room to introduce her. She was wearing a loose black cloak with wide pants and a man's shirt underneath. Her arms were knotted with muscles. Floyd and I were both unsure of what to do next. Salim said Floyd could lie on his stomach on the sofa or on the floor so she could "work" on him. Floyd chose the sofa. He took off his shirt and loosened his belt as requested. A solemn Badreya, who spoke no English, whipped off her cloak and took off her shoes. She stretched her arms as if prepping for a wrestling match and started pounding Floyd's back with her fists. She rhythmically pounded, squeezed, and rubbed. I kept asking Floyd if he was OK with these actions. He nodded.

After about twenty minutes, Floyd said, "That's good. I need to sit up."

"*Kefaya. Shukran, Badreya,*" I thanked her and paid her a pound fifty, as Salim had suggested.

Floyd sat up, drank some lemonade Salim brought him, and pronounced, "My back feels better."

Badreya returned several times for longer sessions.

▲ ▲ ▲

Soliman had many talents. He brought a small radio with him and played it while he worked in the kitchen. I came into the kitchen one morning to ask a how-do-I-say-this-in-Arabic question. Instead, I commented on the music.

"That's Soliman's music, Madame. I play it on *oud*."

He reached for a well-worn black music case tucked under the table. He pulled out a polished, short-necked, pear-shaped stringed instrument. It had no frets and eleven strings. He placed it on his knee and stroked the strings with a long pick. I reveled in the intervals and micro-tones of Middle Eastern music that this instrument produced. Salim told me he composed and played music that was sometimes played on one of the local radio stations. He was very proud of this, even though he received no payment from the stations. When he finished his cooking and housework, he would play the oud. His music became the background to the remainder of our Egyptian experiences.

▲ ▲ ▲

Our third Christmas in Cairo was coming. This year, we had an artificial tree that we had purchased in the American community rummage sale. We wouldn't need to nail it to the parquet floor in the living room, as Salim had engineered last year. Cairo shops began decorating and selling gifts and special candies and pastries. Coptic Christians celebrate Christmas Day on January 7, so the spirit of the holiday season lasts well past December 25. Even though only ten percent of the Egyptian population is Christian, many Egyptians like to celebrate Christmas as a secular holiday.

Groppi's, the Swiss-owned, world-famous coffee shop and bakery, had festive window displays and the most delicious chocolates and ice cream. A trip to this historic shop on Talaat Harb Square was the highlight of our family Christmas preparations.

Troy received a surprise gift on Christmas Eve day. We were walking home from a visit to the Ferrars. As we opened our gate, we could hear whimpering from the yard at the back of the villa. We traced the yipping to a pit half-covered by a chunk of cement and surrounded by bushes. Floyd removed the cement cover and found a pit about two feet deep. At the bottom of the pit was a puppy. Floyd managed to lie on his stomach as he tried to reach the puppy. The stench and the slippery fur of the dog made it difficult. The kids were frantic, and I was afraid of Floyd's exposure to whatever had been in the pit. He finally grabbed the puppy by the nape of its neck. He had retrieved a two- or three-month-old, dirty, smelly dog with fuzzy brown and, possibly, white fur.

"My present!" Troy said. "Sandy Claus brought me a puppy."

Our guess was that someone who knew we were animal lovers had put the puppy in the yard while we were gone. Unfortunately, it had fallen into the pit. We used lots of Rabso soap to wash off both Floyd and the little male puppy. I wrapped the pup in a towel and placed it onto Troy's lap. The kids decided to name it Holly, in the spirit of Christmas.

▲ ▲ ▲

Shortages continued into the 1974 New Year. We decided it was time to take a short vacation during the January school break. We wanted to introduce Bob and Joyce Ferrar and their children to the island of Cyprus. The fun and relaxation started the minute we got on the Cyprus Air plane. We boarded in the middle and then found our seats facing the rear of the plane. The other half of the seats faced forward. Initially, this made the kids feel like they were flying backwards on a carnival ride. Even though it was just an hour and a half flight, we were served delicious omelets, fresh fruit, and little muffins—the first eggs we'd had in months. We had missed both napkins and toilet paper in Cairo, so we surreptitiously stuffed extras in our backpacks and purses.

The Cypriots were just as friendly as we had found them on our first trip to the island. They appeared to be a harmonious blend of Turkish and Greek cultures. The Greek population was approximately half a million compared to the Turkish population of about one hundred and twenty thousand. We quickly became aware of an internal strife between Greek and Turkish Cypriots. Taxi drivers and restaurant owners we conversed with eagerly educated us about the conflict. The two communities had differing political goals. The Greek Cypriot majority wanted union with Greece (Enosis), while the Turkish Cypriot minority opposed this, fearing marginalization of their people. They asked for the division of the island into two parts. This solution was reminiscent of British colonial policies that had encouraged polarization between the two ethnic groups through their divide-and-conquer strategies.

Unfortunately, this would be our last visit to this lovely island. The Turks invaded Cyprus in July of 1974. We had no idea then that Greek Cypriots would become an important part of our lives in later years.

The Goat Herd

Is she-goat or human
        this four-foot woman
        cocooned in black?
No evil eye
        dares pierce
        the prison grate
of plastic charms
        that mask
        her face.
Captive eyes flash
        through veil-slits
        like traffic signals.
leading my bicycle
        zig-zag through
        the maa-ing mass.
Silver shackles bind
        her dusty ankles
        and a bamboo crook
taller than she
        stakes her
        to the sand.
A prisoner
        this goat woman
        of her herd? Her husband?
        Or herself?

17

Amel: Village Wife, City Woman*

"TOMORROW BIG DAY," Amel confided. "Baby cut tomorrow, my baby girl."

The white china plates landed with a dust-stirring thud onto the blue cloth as she hurriedly set the table for lunch in the dining room of the Ferrar's house. Joyce and I chatted in the nearby alcove. Amel, a widow of the 1967 War, had worked for the Ferrars for the past year. During that time, I had encouraged her to tell me the story of her life as Paul and Troy played together at the villa.

Today, she was in a hurry. As soon as she fed the three youngest children and washed the dishes, she would catch a bus to Shoubra, a section of Old Cairo. Amel shared a two-room apartment with her mother-in-law, Aziza, her six-year-old son, Saeed, and her four-year-old daughter, Dina.

What did Amel mean when she said her baby would be "cut" today? This procedure, I learned, was *tahari,* clitoral excision that was considered a rite of passage to womanhood, and a cause for celebration. The excision of pre-pubertal girls was a common practice in her village in the Fayoum, a desert oasis, and her mother-in-law still clung to the village traditions, demanding that her son's wife conform to the "old ways." Amel had disagreed but had little power in the relationship.

Conflict with her mother-in-law began when Amel gave birth to her first baby, a son, and continued as her second child, a daughter, was born. When Amel became a widow, Aziza insisted she wear a

* Adapted from *Seven Egyptian Women,* unpublished manuscript, Rocky Mountain Women's Institute, 1977.

black *melaya* to assume the role of widow and to become the cleaner and cook for the family of four living partly on Amel's small widow's allowance.

Amel's balcony was her window on the world. She would watch her neighbor, a young woman dressed neatly in a Western-style skirt and sweater, leave every morning by herself at six to board a bus that would take her to a job in Ma'adi as a cook for an American family. The neighbor girl seemed alive, busy, and eager to go out into the streets that so intrigued Amel. Despite her mother-in-law's complaints about the neighbor's morals, Amel made a new friend, Mona. Amel found out what it was like to work for an American, how much she made (LE fifteen, about twenty-five dollars a month), and asked her if there might be a job for her with a similar family. A week later, Mona returned with the news that the American university was hiring nanny-maids for new professors' families. Amel asked Aziza's permission to go with Mona to see about the job.

"Good girls don't work as servants. It is *haram*!" Aziza shouted, stomping out of the apartment to fetch her son who lived on the same street.

Amel's brother-in-law listened to his mother, but he argued that Amel could work without dishonoring the family. Since he was beginning to feel the burden of financial support for the family and for his mother, he took Amel's side. Aziza finally gave her permission, but insisted all of Amel's monthly salary would be given to her to manage. She would also have full control over Saeed's and Dina's upbringing. And now, here Amel was, happily working for the Ferrar family. However, there was a continual tug between the old ways of the village represented by her mother-in-law and the new ways of Cairo.

Amel remembered her own excision with pain and fear. She was not certain she wanted her daughter to endure this. However, Aziza insisted that it must be done if Dina was to be a good wife later. Amel agreed, with the concession that the less invasive Egyptian method be used, rather than the Pharaonic or Sudanese-style operation that had been performed on both Amel and her mother when they were small children.

Aziza arranged for the neighborhood midwife to come that night, Thursday, for the excision. She had given Amel LE three to buy a new lime green dress for Dina, the first store-bought dress she had ever had.

"Dina will be a little aroos (bride)—like when she get big and marry," shel explained.

Amel finished washing and draining the dishes, bid a quick goodbye to Joyce and me and hurried to the train that would take her from the tree-lined streets of Ma'adi to the Babelouk Station in the heart of Cairo. Ninety minutes later, she walked down the familiar row of crumbling, sand-colored apartment buildings. Dina and Saeed waved from the balcony as soon as they saw Mama's blue dress pass the pink carcasses hanging in front of the corner butcher shop.

"Mama, my dress! My dress!" shouted Dina, jumping up and down on her sturdy brown legs.

Amel met her children on the stairs and started to unwrap the newspaper around the dress when her mother-in-law snatched it from her.

"You are late, Amel, late! Om Zenouba is coming soon."

Then slapping Dina's outstretched hands, she said, "La-a, Dina, first you must have a bath and then the dress."

Amel did not bother to reply to Aziza but nervously hurried to pour the already-heated water into a plastic tub for Dina's bath. Her mother ordered Saeed out of the apartment and down the street to his uncle's house for the evening. After a quick sponge bath, Semeha was dressed in the new green dress. Her eyes were made up with dark brown and green kohl while her mother rubbed her hands and feet with a paste made of henna. Amel's hands trembled so much that she had to redo the arched curves on Semeha's eyelids. She was barely finished when Om Zenuba pushed open the door.

The woman who heaved herself over the door jamb was a moun-tainous, dark-skinned native of Upper Egypt who, during her fifty years of life, had borne twelve children of her own and delivered hundreds of other babies. Her smile was obscured by missing front teeth. Dina didn't seem to object to the kiss planted on both her cheeks. She had known the neighborhood midwife since the day she was born. Amel stroked Dina's little shoulders under the starchy cotton dress.

"Dina," she whispered, "Om Zenuba will make a little cut down there between your legs, so when you get older, you will be a good wife and able to have a fine husband."

"Will it hurt, Mama? I don't want hurt," she whimpered.

"It will hurt a little bit, Dina, but if you don't cry too much, I'll give you some candy, and you'll get presents too."

By now three other neighbors and Amel's aunt had arrived. The women squatted on the floor against the wall of the combined living room and bedroom, avoiding the mattress laid in the corner of the small room. Dina stood with her mother, holding her hand.

"Come, Dina, it's time. Sit here in this chair," Om Zenuba encouraged. "That's a good girl. Now, your mama and grandma will hold your legs like this," she said, spreading the little girl's legs.

"*La-a,* Mama, *la-a,*" Dina protested, starting to cry.

"Dina, you stop that!" her grandmother shouted. "Quiet! It is God's will, this *tahari.*"

"No, it is not. It is your will," Amel said in a small voice.

"Go, Amel. Go to the kitchen until it is over," her mother ordered. "Amel is a child, a bad child," she said to the gathered neighbors. "Now, let us finish."

Amel's aunt placed a yellow plastic bowl beneath Dina and tightly clasped the little girl's hands. Om Zenub's left hand searched out the tiny clitoris and pinched it, and her right hand made a deft cut with the razor blade.

Dina flinched and screamed, "Mama! Mama!"

Om Zenuba flicked the tiny bit of flesh into the pan, which now held the blood from Dina's wound.

"Come now, you are a woman. You become a woman. You become a bride," chanted the women.

Amel came from the kitchen, her face stained with tears and drew Dina close to her while the chanting continued to drown out her daughter's sobs.

"Bring her the groom now. Bring her a penis. She is ready for intercourse." Incantations from the Qur'an interspersed the chants and punctuated by the high shrill cries of joy, *zaghareet.*

While her mother lit fresh sticks of incense to scare away the *djinn* and the evil eye, Dina applied raw egg and green henna to Dina's wound. Om Zenuba then tied the little girl's legs together and carried her to a place of honor on the stained mattress in the corner of the room.

Amel propped Dina up on a pillow and gave her the promised stick of molasses candy and a small sesame cake. Dina grasped the candy in her hands but couldn't stop the sobbing that shook her chest under the tear-stained green dress.

"*Maalesh,* Dina. Never mind."

Amel's words seemed to quiet her.

Aziza took over the role of hostess, serving tea, candy, and popcorn to the guests and sprinkling them with perfume. Everyone congratulated Dina, and Amel presented her with a pink plastic doll and a brightly colored book about Aladdin.

From seven to fifteen days after the *tahari,* Dina would be regarded as healed. Her legs would remain tied together for only one or two days. To give her strength and encourage fertility, she would be fed chicken or pigeon broth and maybe a bit of lentil soup. While her wound healed, she would be treated like a bride or a woman in childbirth.

As Amel sat beside her daughter on the mattress, she remembered her own excision, which took place when she was seven years old. Her operation was the "old-fashioned" or Pharaonic, method in which the clitoris, labia minora, and labia majora were excised. The healing process provided scar tissue for complete closure of the vulva, except for a small urination orifice, which was kept open by a match. It also required another operation to open the vulva before marriage. Dina's operation was a simple excision, which would eliminate the necessity for a second excision at marriage. This change toward moderation was justified by a hadith, (the sayings, actions, and approvals of the Prophet Muhammad: "It is *sunna* (the recommended practice) to cut a small part but not all." Changing attitudes were also reflected in the frequent comment that the simple Egyptian method permitted the wife greater pleasure in sexual intercourse.

Dina knew nothing about the history of clitoral excision, nor could she verbalize her conflicting feelings about the excision of her daughter. But she did have the freedom to feel, to feel pity for the four-year-old and her fear and pain, to feel anger at her mother for forcing the excision upon her, and to feel relief that the event was over.

▲ ▲ ▲

During the 1970s, approximately ninety-five to ninety-seven percent of Egyptian women underwent female excision, according to UNICEF and Demographic and Health Surveys.[1] Women who practiced it cited several reasons for the procedure. First, it was a religious obligation prescribed in Prophet Mohamed's *hadith*. The operation symbolically purified the child, making possible her future participation in prayers. In addition, it was a preventive measure that enhanced cleanliness.

"When the child begins to scratch himself, that is the time to arrange for circumcision" was a common response.

Amel's mother-in-law told her the operation made the woman "like the good soil of the Nile." In other words, it promoted fertility and health. Some believed that without circumcision, a degree of completeness of manhood or womanhood would be missing. This was also implied in the notion that the operation prepared the person to enter marriage, thus the celebratory chant by the women at Dina's circumcision: "You become a woman. You become a bride."

Much to my consternation, the chief reason for female excision concerned chastity. Women who were uncircumcised were considered oversexed and, therefore, apt to be unfaithful and unchaste in their character. This sexual wildness and lack of control was centered in the clitoris. Extremists argued the only way to blunt the sexual lack of control and preserve a woman's chastity was through female excision.

Today, this harmful cultural practice is recognized as a violation of human rights and reflects systemic discrimination rather than any character traits of the women subjected to it. It is practiced on women and girls, often without their consent, because of societal norms, traditions, and gender inequality.

Female genital mutilation (FGM), as it is appropriately called today, is still widespread in Egypt.

▲ ▲ ▲

However, it is increasingly condemned throughout much of North and East Africa. According to the Egyptian Family Health Survey in 2021, eighty-six percent of Egyptian married women between the ages of fifteen to forty-nine had undergone FGM, with seventy-four percent of them by doctors; however, there had been a positive change in women's attitudes about circumcision, with only thirteen percent of mothers intending to circumcise their daughters in the future compared to about thirty-five percent in 2014. Despite the outlawing of FGM in 2008 and increasing jail sentences for practitioners and family members involved, the practice remains prevalent in certain populations.[2]

▲ ▲ ▲

"*Ya*, Amel, come and help serve your guests!" Aziza ordered as she boiled more tea in the kitchen.

"No, Mama," Amel said. "I want to read this book of Aladdin to Dina."

"Read?"Aziza said. "Since when did you learn to read?"

Amel looked up at her mother-in-law. and in a quiet but defiant voice said, "I am learning, Mama. And Dina will learn too."

Amel

"Today big day," Amel tells me.
"Baby cut today, my little girl."
This nineteen-year-old nanny,
mother, widow of Suez
will give her child today
for circumcision rites.
"When she get big
she be good wife,
En sh'allah."

The Ironing Lady

Gamalat, the makwagi,
came late today
her son of seven months
died last night
just like three other
babies, too, had gone.
"Maybe it was my milk
or just God's will,
but ma'alesh," she said.

18

Coca Cola and Levi Jeans

AS 1974 ROLLED into Cairo, a sense of excitement was in the air—both politically and socio-economically. In January, the First Egyptian-Israeli Disengagement Agreement was signed. It called for a ceasefire and the withdrawal of Israeli forces from parts of the Sinai Peninsula, which had been occupied since the Six-Day War in 1967. President Sadat had initiated diplomatic moves aimed at stabilizing the region and improving relations with Western countries, particularly the United States. His open door policy led to American companies looking to capitalize on new opportunities in Egypt. American oil companies, construction, banking, and consumer goods rushed to establish a presence in the country.

When we traveled down the Corniche and visited the shops in Cairo, and even in Ma'adi, we saw American, British, and other Western products on billboards and store shelves. Egyptians with money bought Sony Televisions, RCA appliances, Ford and Peugeot cars, Coca-Cola, Cadbury Chocolates, Levi Jeans, and Marks & Spencer Clothing. We could even purchase familiar brands like Colgate toothpaste and Gillette razors at Gomaa Brothers Grocery in Ma'adi.

Posters of President Sadat showed him in military whites with medals on his chest rather than the two-piece safari suits that he had sported when he first took office.

Changes occurred at AUC too. Sadat returned full control of the university to the board of trustees. The university experienced increased enrollment and diversity. There was more demand for higher education, as Egypt's economy began to open.

This, in turn, created new opportunities for educated professionals. The influx of foreign businesses and expatriates into Cairo led to a more diverse student body. The emphasis on development studies and public policy programs was intended to address Egypt's socio-economic challenges. Floyd's communications program hoped to put more emphasis on freedom of the press and ethics in journalism. His Communication of Innovations book enjoyed increased sales of mimeographed copies. In May, Floyd was honored with an invitation, along with journalists and public policy officials, to join Henry Kissinger on a Nile riverboat cruise during the US secretary of state's second "shuttle diplomacy" visit. Although the agenda was heavily scripted with archaeological information, Floyd met influential figures in the Egyptian government and had informative conversations with members of the international press. Kissinger impressed Floyd as very formal and intimidating. He was not the type of person you would chat with, Floyd said, noting that Kissinger's German accent slowed down his speech and made listeners more attentive.

▲ ▲ ▲

Two side-by-side stories in the student newspaper, *The Caravan*, proved that the university was coming into the modern age but also experiencing post-war problems. The most important story was AUC's acquisition of an Associated Press News Agency wire service for use as a training tool and for information purposes. The second story revealed the more mundane concerns that interfered with academic pursuits.

"Student Complaints about Toilet Paper" was the headline. Since the beginning of the Spring semester students had been complaining about shortages of soap and toilet paper in bathrooms on campus.

"The university has applied for fifty-eight hundred rolls of paper from the director of Workers and Business. We get only three hundred toilet paper rolls per month for the fifty-eight toilets in both campuses," the director of facilities said. "No solution is in sight because it is a nationwide problem."

▲ ▲ ▲

A big event in our lives was the arrival of US President Richard Nixon on June 12 after extensive shuttle diplomacy preparations by Henry Kissinger with both Arab and Israeli leaders. President Sadat and the first lady greeted him at the airport, supported by thousands of enthusiastic Egyptians. Missy got to experience the excitement because she was in a delegation of CAC students transported there with American flags in hand to wave when President Nixon exited Air Force One. When she brought her souvenir flag home, we noticed it had only forty-eight stars on it. It probably had been packed in someone's closet for more than twenty years.

A *Time Magazine* article described Nixon's arrival as a "triumph of sorts" with the "huzzas and hosannas falling like sweet rain."

Nixon said he had "received the most tumultuous welcome any American president has received anywhere in the world."

More than a million people packed the streets and city squares, holding signs that read "We Trust Nixon!" and chanting "Nik-son. Nik-son. Nik-son."

I was posted on a second-floor balcony in the business district, along with several other Associated Press reporters, to observe and take notes on the official parade. We discovered that most Cairenes lining the streets had been paid several *piastres* to wave signs and shout their welcomes.

In addition to international diplomacy, domestic politics evolved. Sadat's government faced challenges related to conditions following the war, including inflation and food shortages. In response to these issues, he implemented the infitah that encouraged foreign investment and reduced state control over certain sectors of the economy.

Not everyone was happy with these reforms and their implications for Egyptian society. Arab nationalist sentiments favored resistance against Israel rather than negotiation. Sadat cracked down on the dissenting voices, targeting leftist movements that opposed his policies and peace overtures toward Israel. This included arrests and increased surveillance of political activists.

The Egyptian government had strict control over media narratives. Our foreign correspondent friends were required to register with authorities and could face censorship on sensitive topics, such as internal politics or criticisms of the government. Journalists were expected to adhere to certain guidelines that aligned with state interests, which limited their ability to report freely on controversial issues and criticism of the government. When they overstepped the boundaries, they could be arrested and expelled from the country. One example that served as a warning to other journalists was the expulsion of John McCarthy, an American journalist working for the Associated Press. His reporting was "deemed unfavorable by the government."

Arrests were part of a broader pattern of repression aimed at silencing critical voices in the media. Sadat was maintaining a tight grip on dissent within the country while trying to open Egypt to Western influences, economically and politically.

The atmosphere in the Journalism and Mass Communications classes at AUC was constrained and discussions were tempered by an awareness of the political risks involved. Floyd's graduate program was composed of students from radio, television, and print journalism. Whispering in small group discussions was a common way of communicating their underlying sense of anger. Any overt critical stance could attract unwanted attention from authorities. The university administration itself had to navigate these tensions carefully. While it supported academic freedom, it also had to consider potential repercussions from the government.

▲ ▲ ▲

It was time for the Shoemaker family to experience the growing international atmosphere in Cairo. CAC had a school holiday, so we decided to visit the Omar Khayyam Hotel for lunch and a swim for the kids. The hotel was on Gezira Island in Zamalek. Floyd and I were interested in seeing the historic building, which was constructed as the Gezirah Palace for Khedive Ismail Pasha in 1869. It was now a popular venue for various international events and guests from around the world.

The taxi driver who arrived at our villa was not the familiar Saeed the Spy. We hadn't seen him since a week or two before the war, and we missed his sense of humor and informative conversation. Our new driver was a bulky, grumpy man who chewed gum in rhythm with the loud music on his radio. When we reached Gezira, the taxi stopped in front of a grand European palace. A doorman in a dark blue uniform and a red Turkish *tarboosh* helped us out of the taxi. We didn't feel appropriately dressed for the luxury of the hotel until we noticed the variety of people in the candle-lit dining area. There were United Nations soldiers, women in sundresses, businessmen in suits, and children carrying swim bags, so they could visit the pool after lunch. Sonja was pleased to use the French she had been studying and helped us to make choices from the menu. Missy chose her favorite Croque-Monsieur, a grilled ham and cheese sandwich, and Troy joined her order only if we hurried so he could swim. After lunch, we sat in the lush garden at the edge of the pool where we could watch the kids.

A tanned, young blond man sat down next to us and introduced himself as Timothy from Ottawa, Canada.

"Are you American? I heard you speaking English. I wondered if you're on a tour."

We introduced ourselves as Americans, Coloradans to be exact, and explained why we were in Cairo. Timothy said he was with the

United Nations Emergency Force (UNEF), a new peacekeeping operation that was monitoring the ceasefire between Israel and Egypt. He was on leave from the Suez Canal region, where his mission was de-mining. This was the first we had heard of explosive devices placed by Israeli forces to prevent Egyptian troops from crossing into Sinai and to secure Israeli-held territories. Timothy said the mines were "scattered like rice at a wedding" but killing hundreds of Egyptian children and adults. The use of mines could have lasting impacts on the post-war recovery effort to ensure civilian safety and restore normalcy to an important region of the country.

A lovely afternoon had come to an end. Time to hail a taxi home to Ma'adi. The children changed into street clothes and packed up their swim equipment. When we left the Omar Khayyam, the doorman was not at the entrance to hail us a taxi, so we decided to walk about two blocks to a busier street, where we could find transportation. We stood at the curb, near a stop sign, to look down the street for a cab.

A nearby school had just let out, so the sidewalk was packed with kids in rumpled grey uniforms ready for freedom and a release of their energy. We stood out like a poster family on one of the new billboards: rich Americans, long-haired girls, and a little boy in a Disney T-shirt. We were a funny-looking, vulnerable group of foreigners. Before we knew it, junior high kids surrounded us, laughing and asking questions. Then, one of the girls came up behind Missy and gave a tug on her hair. One of the boys poked a finger on Troy's T-shirt.

"*Eh, da?*"

Troy used his favorite Arabic word, "*Emshi!*" Get away from me!

He kicked the boy in the shin and turned around to protect Missy from the girl who had pulled her hair.

"*La-a! Kiff! Insarif!* No! Stop. Go away!" Those were the only worlds I could muster.

We were all in panic mode. No adult was to be found in the

crowd, and no taxis were in the traffic speeding by. The crowd of kids grew. A small VW pulled up to us through the crowd. The window rolled down, and a lady with an Australian accent said, "It looks like you're in trouble. Get in. All of you. You can sit on laps."

We had been rescued by an Australian couple, who took us several miles to a taxi stand where we found a safe ride home to Ma'adi. *Al hamdu lillah*! Praise be to God!

The Blind Man

Who's this
on my front step
folded
in a tattered
package
no teeth left
no eyes
no shoes
head tied on with knotted rags?

"Madame, ana mish kwayess,"
a beggar's priest
crossing first his heart
and then his clouded eyes.

"Shwayya baksheesh, min fadlik?"
his dry lips brush my hand
a gallant wooing piastres
from my purse.

"Rabbina ya khaliki, thank you. shukran!"
Now a beggar
grateful for the coins
he rises,
tapping out his way
from house to house.

19

Weaving Together the Threads

AS A SMALL child in Longmont, Colorado, I watched my Danish grandmother crochet. It was fascinating to watch her crochet hook move swiftly back and forth as she interlocked colorful loops of thread or wool into squares. Like magic, those squares became doilies, scarves, or even blankets. As I look back at our last full year in Cairo, I can see the threads of my life intertwining to shape the person I have become. Starting in high school as editor of the Denver West High *Rodeo,* my goal was to be a writer, particularly a journalist. Floyd and I met and fell in love as seniors and studied together on scholarships at Colorado State University. As the semesters progressed, he realized that journalism was also a good match for him. We edited the college newspaper together with his goal of master's and PhD degrees in communication. To facilitate this, I took teaching jobs along the way plus, of course, combining this with starting a family.

We moved eight times in our first fifteen years of marriage, sometimes shuttling back and forth between Colorado State and Michigan State for his PhD. I became an expert at the settling-in process after each uprooting. It was difficult to develop my writing life and be a good wife and mother. Journalism had been my chosen profession, but teaching English was a practical way of supporting our family while Floyd studied. I enjoyed teaching, but I still had an urge to write. In each place we moved, I found ways to work part-time for local newspapers, write columns, and compose poetry, but these bits and pieces of experience made it difficult to develop my writing skills.

My Cairo experience gave me the opportunity to take the threads from the past and weave them into a meaningful fabric. I was not in Cairo to change and develop the country. That was Floyd's goal. I was there to live within the culture—to observe and record what I saw. Hand in hand with this purpose was to give our children a broader view of the world and its cultures. I was given the opportunity to teach at an oil company, a high school for international students, and a university. Throughout these three years, I had written free-lance articles for the *Lansing State Journal* and the *Cleveland Plain Dealer*, feature articles for the Associated Press, and poetry about Egypt, which was printed by the AUC Press. The little volume, "Ma'alesh: Verses from Egypt," was sold in the Hilton and Sheraton Hotel bookstores, with all proceeds going to a charity sponsored by the Ma'adi Women's Club. These experiences came together to take me in a new direction in this final year in Cairo. I wanted to explore the lives of the women I had met.

▲ ▲ ▲

American women were striving for equality with men. When Floyd and I married in 1955, the ideal wife should maintain the house, prepare meals, take care of the children, and help them with their homework. She was expected to do the dishes and laundry while remaining sexy and elegant. This started to change in the 1960s when our children were born. The '60s feminists demanded equal pay for equal work, the end to domestic violence, an opportunity to take managerial jobs, an end to sexual harassment, and sharing the responsibility of work and child rearing with their husbands.

Now here I was in the early 1970s: living in a villa in a developing country with servants to fix meals, wash and iron the family clothes (albeit in a wringer washer and a 1940 iron), running the household and our children's scholastic lives, and still with some time on my hands to pursue my writing. I wasn't by myself in these endeavors. I was fortunate to know accomplished women who interrupted careers in the States to accompany their husbands to Cairo. Were they able to pursue their careers? Did the Cairo experience enhance those careers?

▲ ▲ ▲

Olga Miniclier was the wife of Christopher "Kit" Miniclier, Associated Press bureau chief in Cairo. Olga was a gifted professional artist trained at the Munich Academy of Fine Arts. Her artistic talents were diverse; she created portraits and landscapes that garnered international recognition through exhibitions and awards. In Cairo, her focus was on portraits of the common men and women of the city. She had a daily schedule of sketching and painting. Her works were celebrated for their beauty and emotional depth, and they sold well to the expatriate community and to upper-class Egyptians.

Her memorial tribute fifty years after the Cairo experience illustrates the impact her overseas life had on her career:

▲ ▲ ▲

During these years of global exploration, Olga developed a remarkable ability to connect with people from diverse cultures through engaging conversations (she spoke seven languages), her sharp intellect, and her exceptional culinary skills. Her paintings continue to bring joy to viewers worldwide even after her passing. Through her art, she left behind an enduring legacy that reflects her talent for capturing life's essence on canvas.

▲ ▲ ▲

I became friends with Bonnie Jo Hunt, the wife of AUC professor Dr. Lawrence Hunt. Bonnie Jo was a prominent Native American opera singer and activist, known for her contributions to both the arts and the Native American community. A Hunkpapa Sioux and descendant of Chief Mad Bear, who fought in the Battle of Little BigHorn, she grew up on a remote Sioux reservation. Bonnie Jo gained recognition as an operatic singer, performing with the San Francisco Opera and Opera Southwest in Albuquerque. Unlike traditional operatic performances, she focused on American Indian music.

In Cairo, it was not easy for Bonnie Jo to find a niche for her unique talents, but she occasionally performed at small gatherings for the Ma'adi community. Her operatic career was put on hold until she and Larry returned to the States. In 1979, Bonnie Jo founded Artists of Indian America, a performing arts organization aimed at raising self-esteem among Native American students by show-casing performances from professional artists—both Indian and non-Indian.

▲ ▲ ▲

Her work continues to inspire efforts toward inclusivity within classical music while celebrating the richness of Native American heritage, reflecting her commitment to using art as a means of empowerment for Indigenous communities," according to a Los Angeles Times *review.*

▲ ▲ ▲

Anne Marie Harrison was best known to me as Justin's mom and the wife of Bill Harrison, Ford Foundation executive and AUC administrator. However, before she and Bill began their African and

Middle Eastern sojourn, Anne Marie had achieved a significant career in musical performance and education. She studied at the Institute of Music in Philadelphia and performed at Carnegie Hall with the Philadelphia Orchestra. Before her international focus, she was the head of the Voice Department at the University of Corpus Christi in Texas, where she taught music and continued to perform.

In Cairo, Ann Marie balanced care for her two children, management of the household, an active social life, and an occasional vocal performance. She also participated in the local cultural scene by supporting local arts organizations such as the Cairo Opera Company. She expanded her career as the family's life in Cairo became more permanent. She and her husband established a publishing company and began publishing an English language magazine *Egypt Today,* followed by *Business Today Egypt.* When Bill died, she continued the publications.

▲ ▲ ▲

In 1974, Egyptian women in Cairo started pushing for more participation in public life and job opportunities. Women were becoming aware of the need for equality with men and quietly advocating for change. Numerous women exemplified these changes, ranging from Amel, the village woman who endured the practice of genital mutilation on her daughter, to Jehan Sadat, the first lady of Egypt, who actively promoted women's rights and social reforms.

I had the honor of meeting Jehan Sadat in April 1974. I was invited, along with about twenty-five other American women, to have tea with Egypt's first lady following a bus tour of two sites she was developing in Nasr City: the SOS Children's Village and the Faith and Hope Rehabilitation Center for war veterans medical and rehabilitation services. The Ma'adi Women's Club was a major contributor to the Villages through money raised on special projects.

After our tour, we returned to the presidential residence, Ittihadiya Palace, the former residence of King Farouk. The palace was not only a residence but also a center for political activity and diplomacy. President Sadat hosted numerous state functions, meetings with foreign dignitaries, and significant events here. It was common for the first lady to host tea parties or receptions at the palace. She often invited women from various sectors, such as politics, academia, art, and business to these gatherings. We were hosted in an elegant salon that opened into a garden of spring tulips, crocus, and daffodils. We sat in a circle of individual tea tables including Jehan, who could have been just another guest at the event. She was wearing an aqua silk blouse and a below-the-knee black skirt. Simple but stylish. Waiters produced an array of fruits, pastries, and hors d'oeuvres while Jehan chatted with us about her efforts to promote women's rights and education in Egypt.

How did this unassuming, quiet woman in our tea circle become the first lady of Egypt? She was born in Cairo as the child of an upper-middle-class family of an Egyptian surgeon and a British music teacher mother. According to her father's wishes, she was raised as a Muslim, but she attended a Coptic Christian high school. She met her future husband, Anwar Sadat, at her fifteenth birthday party shortly after his release from prison, where he served two and a half years for resistance activities that helped to depose King Farouk. She and Sadat married two years later, after hesitation from her parents to their daughter marrying a jobless revolutionary. She gave birth to three daughters and a son.

Jehan had begun her work for women's rights in the years before she became first lady. She was vocal in condemning female genital mutilation and played a crucial role in the 1960s in the formation of a co-operative in the village of Talla in the Nile Delta that helped local women become skilled in sewing and, therefore, economically independent of their husbands.

"Over half our population are women, Anwar," she told her husband, as she stated in her biography, *A Woman of Egypt.* "Egypt will not be a democracy until women are as free as men."

Education was another cornerstone of Jehan Sadat's advocacy. She believed that education was essential for women's empowerment. She was also a graduate student at the time of our tea, earning an MA degree in Arabic literature and comparative literature at Cairo University. She later received a PhD.

It was exciting to follow the efforts we heard about at tea to their fruition after we returned to the States into what became known as "Jehan's Laws," enacted in 1979. These laws granted women the right to divorce, allowing them to leave unhappy or abusive marriages; custody rights, which ensured women could retain custody of their children after divorce; and financial support, granting rights to alimony and child support. These legislative changes were a significant step toward gender equality in Egypt and empowered women to assert their rights within the family structure.

After her husband's assassination in 1981, Jehan faced a challenging political climate in Egypt under Hosni Mubarak's presidency. Mubarak's government did not prioritize or expand upon the progressive women's rights agenda that Jehan had championed during her time as first lady. Given the circumstances surrounding her husband's assassination by extremists opposed to his policies (including his peace treaty with Israel), Jehan faced personal safety concerns that limited her ability to engage directly in activism within Egypt. This did not stop her from changing the world's image of Arab women. She was a visiting professor at the University of Maryland, and she hosted and participated in conferences throughout the world concerning women's issues, children's welfare, and peace. She died in Egypt in 2021 at the age of eighty-seven.

▲ ▲ ▲

My friend, Shahinaz Talaat, inspired me with her courage, academic achievements, and belief in freedom of expression. I met Shahinaz when she was a graduate student in Floyd's communications program. She invited our family to her home to welcome us to Cairo and meet her husband, businessman Saleh Al Fahmy, and their sons. They helped us navigate through the twists and turns of our Cairo adventure, always willing to give us insight into the culture, to assist us in finding services, and to support us in challenging times. They are the friends who responded to Missy's broken leg by bringing her the especially important tape recorder that entertained her for hours each day. Shahinaz and her husband also visited Floyd in the hospital and at home when he was ill.

After we left Cairo, Shahinaz was severely injured in a car crash on the road to Alexandria. Despite her injuries and difficulty with mobility and speech, she continued to pursue her education and became Dr. Shahinaz, a professor at Cairo University. She was staunch in her beliefs in women's rights. When conservative Islamist groups gained influence in Egyptian society in the '80s and '90s, women were required to wear niqab. a traditional veil that covered the hair and face, except for the eyes. Shahinaz refused to wear a hijab while teaching her university communication classes.

"How can you communicate without seeing your facial expressions?" was her response to complaints.

Her marriage to Saleh opened my eyes to the Egyptian legal system's view of women's rights in marriage. Shahinaz explained to me that she and Saleh had signed a marriage contract that allowed her to pursue her education through the PhD and to work in her chosen field. In Islam, marriage is viewed as a *nikah,* a contract between the two parties. It is governed by principles derived from the Qur'an and the *hadith.* According to Islamic jurisprudence, a husband and a wife have the right to negotiate terms that suit their individual circumstances. This includes provisions related to education, career aspirations, and other personal freedoms. Islamic scholars agree that a husband cannot unilaterally impose restrictions on his wife's ability to work or study unless these restrictions are mutually agreed upon during the marriage contract negotiation. What an important factor to settle before any marriage, Muslim, Christian, or other.

▲ ▲ ▲

I saw so much hope of progress toward Egyptian women's rights in the women I knew and wrote about. Today, I am saddened by the statistics. The sexual harassment that infuriated me fifty years ago has been a major factor in the lack of progress Egyptian women have made toward women's rights to safety, dignity, and equal opportunities.

Today, public spaces continue to be unsafe for women. Harassment by males restricts women's access to education, employment opportunities, and civic participation. According to research group Arab Barometer, in 2020, over 1.7 million women reportedly experienced harassment in public transportation annually, which can stop them from commuting to work or school. While initiatives such as awareness campaigns and self-defense training have been introduced, they address only part of the issue. Gender-based violence toward women is deeply ingrained in Egyptian society. The lack of effective legal enforcement further heightens the problem, as only a small fraction of victims report harassment incidents. Today, Cairo is considered one of the most dangerous megacities for women, influenced by factors such as lack of protection from sexual violence, harmful cultural practices, and limited access to healthcare and finance.[1]

Several high-profile incidents have drawn international attention to this crisis: In February 2011, during the Egyptian uprising at Tahrir Square, reports emerged of mass sexual assaults against female protesters. A video taken during celebrations for President Abdel Fattah el-Sisi's inauguration went viral online. Lara Logan, a CBS

News correspondent, became separated from her team and was attacked by a mob of approximately two to three hundred men. She endured a brutal and sustained sexual assault and beating before being rescued by a group of women and soldiers.[2]

Despite these challenges, there have been ongoing efforts by activists and organizations to combat sexual harassment and violence. While progress has been slow, these are steps toward creating safer environments where women can exercise their full rights without fear or intimidation.

▲ ▲ ▲

The stories told to me by the women I met ignited my passion for writing about women of diverse cultures, ages, and backgrounds. What is so compelling about these narratives? Women have played a crucial role in passing down oral traditions, folklore, and personal stories that hold within them cultural values, beliefs, and experiences. Women's stories also reflect the nuances of daily life, family dynamics, and community relationships. Identity, social justice, and personal struggle are human experiences shared by all of us. In his university classes, Floyd often lectured about "change agents," individuals who promote change within a social system by influencing the attitudes, beliefs, and behaviors of others. He and I never had the opportunity to talk about women's roles, but I think he would have agreed that women's stories serve as vital indicators of changes within culture and society. As shifts toward gender equality or changes in family structures evolve, women's narratives often reflect these transformations. In other words, women's stories are not just personal anecdotes; they are powerful reflections of cultural heritage and societal evolution. They hold the potential to challenge existing norms while fostering understanding across diverse communities. If we value women's stories, we acknowledge the critical role women play in shaping our collective history and future.

Song of Celebration

From childhood, they unfold
slender, sleek, and bright
like butterflies in sun warmth
every trial flight
underlined by newborn grace
"I am me!"
these wide-eyed creatures sing.

From yesterday they move
brown legs strolling free
walking, running through their world
calling all to see
beneath the mirror's reflection
"I am me!"
they shout at passersby.

I am dreamer, I am realist,
I belong, yet am alone
I am pupil, teacher, son, and father
soldier, child, a friend, and lover
and at my best
I am a happy "yes"
said to myself,
"I am me!"

20

Drinking the Water of the Nile

THE SIX A.M. call to prayer crept through the shutters of our bedroom window. It reminded me that I was still awake, and it was time to get up. Planning and worrying occupied my mind throughout the night. Our departure from Cairo was drawing closer. At the top of our worry list was the lack of a job for Floyd at a US university. Once again, Colorado was our dream, but we realized it might not be possible initially because flying to the States for necessary interviews was too costly. Bob Ferrar had already returned in June to his position at Cleveland State after fulfilling his two-year contract with AUC. He felt confident that Cleveland State University would offer Floyd a position, but so far we'd had no response to the documents Floyd sent. Another possibility was Washington State University in Vancouver, Canada, but it required an interview by March 1. *En sha'allah,* something would be firmed up before we left.

As much as I wanted to return to the States, I realized that all of us would have to go through a cultural adjustment process. The university brochure called it "re-entry culture shock." It certainly wouldn't be as difficult as the initial culture shock of Cairo, but it wasn't like we were returning from a vacation or a year abroad. We had lived in Cairo for four years. We would want to share our adventures with relatives and old and new friends, but would anyone really want to hear our stories? Would we be able to adjust to new housing, new routines, and new schools? Had I forgotten how to drive a car? Would Troy get the attention he had enjoyed as a first grader at CAC? Would Sonja and Missy fit into the teenage culture of the States, or would they even want to? This was one of my biggest concerns.

Teenage life in Cairo was much simpler than what I had read about or seen when we were on home leave. We would be in the States for the beginning of the 1975–76 school year. Sonja would be fourteen years old and Missy almost thirteen. They had led an enjoyable but sheltered existence here in Cairo. The conservative cultural norms and traditional Muslim values set limits on the way they dressed and how they behaved. These challenges were skillfully mediated by their attendance at CAC. Sonja and Missy weren't just attending CAC; they were an integral part of the international school's family. Their experience supported the transition into adolescence by meeting in small classes where it was easy to make friends, receive individual attention, gain respect for the host culture and the diverse cultures of the students, and enjoy a full schedule of extracurricular activities and sports.

Being the parents of a teen in Cairo also had its advantages. I knew of only one expat teen who drove a car. Driving in Cairo was hazardous enough for adults, let alone for a teenager with a new driver's license. Dating without a car was a bonus from a parent's viewpoint. No worry about accidents, missing curfews, or parking at the pyramids at midnight. What would you do here if you were allowed to date a boy? You could walk to a Ma'adi Club movie or a friend's house, have your parents drive you to an evening dance party at a villa, or, if you were an embassy kid, enlist your driver to take you to a party at a home in the community. Chances are there would be no liquor served because it wasn't for sale in Cairo; however, many expat communities had their own stashes. Your parents would be supervising your activities, but their responsibilities would be much lighter here than they would be at home. I hoped Floyd and I were ready for our new role as parents of two teenage girls in the United States.

▲ ▲ ▲

Leaving Cairo required many tasks, both practical and emotional. The practical ones included finishing the classes I was teaching, deciding what was essential to take with us, and interfacing with the university for packing and shipping our personal belongings to Denver or another destination. Floyd planned to donate more than fifty mass communication and journalism books to the AUC library. His larger legacy was the vibrant graduate program he had helped to create and the talented students who had completed the program. He continued to be busy with teaching classes, in addition to producing numerous progress reports and recommendations for the future of the master's program. Even though there were several months left until our departure, his devoted students were already giving him gifts and inviting us to goodbye events in their homes.

Emotional tasks were more difficult. These involved graciously leaving our many friends, trusted household helpers, colleagues, and students. There were so many people we loved here, coupled with the fact that we might not see some of them again. We started gathering contact information for those we hoped would be in the States in the future.

And not to forget our beloved pets: Holly, Snoopy, Patches, and Richard. Troy desperately wanted to take his dog, Holly, with us. I found out she would have to be in quarantine for 30 days in London and then, if she passed the no-disease screening, she could be shipped on to our destination. I told Troy that Holly would be happier staying right here in the villa, if possible. The university had already placed the next occupants of our villa, the Imhoof family. I was able to write to them about our menagerie of pets. Happily, they also loved animals and promised they would do their best to take care of them.

I could not leave Egypt without tangible memories of our four years here. During the past two years, I purchased meaningful objects that would bridge the gap between Cairo and the US. Shahinaz helped me to find a beautiful, three-hundred-year-old mashrabiya screen, authenticate it, and strike a bargain for it. She also suggested

I meet a renowned brass engraver in the Moussky. He engraved a large, oval brass tray for me to use as a coffee table. With his tiny hand tools, he etched the intricacies of a Persian folk tale replete with a king, a royal court, animals, and birds. I visited him for tea and a view of his progress each month for four months until he finished the tray.

Floyd didn't enjoy shopping and bargaining, but he greatly appreciated the photography of one of his accomplished students, a prominent photojournalist, Mohamed El-Shahed.

Mohamed gave "Dr. Floyd" one of his street scene photographs, and we purchased several other large framed photos of various aspects of Egyptian life. One of my favorite places to visit was the Wissa Wassef Art Center in Harrania Village near the Giza pyramids. Children there learned the art of weaving to create intricate tapestries using their imagination without prior sketches or plans. I bought a charming tree of life weaving that a ten-year-old girl had created. I particularly cherished the folk-art figures of the people we saw on the street every day. I couldn't resist the painted wood and molded clay figures of fruit sellers, mothers in melayas, street sweepers, and comic figures engaged in arguments or laughing at jokes. I hoped these Egyptian mementos would keep our Cairo life fresh in our minds and hearts.

▲ ▲ ▲

Even though our focus was on closing the chapters of our domestic and professional lives in Cairo, we could not ignore the political backdrop to our activities. Discussions were ongoing about the withdrawal of Israeli forces from parts of the Sinai Peninsula occupied during the war. Sadat's approach was controversial domestically; he faced opposition from various factions within Egypt who were skeptical about making concessions to Israel. The political climate was tense. Sadat was trying to balance national pride with practical diplomacy aimed at economic recovery and stability for Egypt. Our Egyptian friends grappled with both hope for peace and anxiety over potential instability resulting from the president's policies. The atmosphere in this city of almost eight million people was charged with anticipation about future developments in Egyptian-Israeli relations. In September 1975, just a few months after we left, negotiations between Egypt and Israel culminated in the Sinai Interim Agreement.

▲ ▲ ▲

Our favorite getaways were also in turmoil. Luckily, we had experienced Christmas break in Cyprus in January before Turkish forces had invaded in July. At that point, they captured about three percent of the island. Following a breakdown in peace negotiations and further escalation, Turkey launched a second phase in August, resulting in the capture of about thirty-six percent of the island, when a ceasefire was negotiated.

I will always remember our friendly taxi guide, Khalil, as the face of Lebanon. In April of this year, 1975, civil war broke out. The roots of this conflict could be traced back to various socio-political tensions among Lebanon's diverse religious communities, economic disparities, and influences from neighboring countries. Peace would not arrive in Lebanon until 1990.

▲ ▲ ▲

As we approached our departure on June 11, I reflected on the impact of our four-year sojourn. Personally, I had grown in confidence, decision-making, and a strong sense of purpose. I could sense that it would be a pivotal point in my life. The often-repeated phrase: "He who drinks from the water of the Nile is destined to taste it again" meant more to me and our family than wishing to visit Cairo in the future. We had absorbed the history and culture that oozed through the pores of the city and connected us with the land and the people.

Life Is the River

Life is the River
and the River is life
mother of the people
and suckler of the child
mover and quickener
with Promethean power.

Already mighty
from Uganda, she flows
white roiling waters
to be wed in Sudan
by the blue torrent
of its mate, Ethiope.

Flowing, cascading
into Egypt, she moves,
drowning its history
with a swallow and surge
spreading like spilt milk
over Nubian towns,

mirroring vain Ramses
chopped up in blocks
jig-sawed by Frenchmen
and Italians and Swedes
reborn to glory,
as his fate has decreed.

Life is the River
and she must be contained
Saad el Aali draws together her strength
harnessing, saving
from the fat years to lean,

past near-drowned Philae
the last refuge of Isis,
guided from Aswan
to Kom Ombo, Edfu,
she gives her life's blood
to the meek fellahiin.

Young wife of Esna
heel-squats down on the bank, belly protruding
and scoops up from the mud mouthfuls of magic
to protect her from pain.

Liquid like sand slides
ever onward the stream
past lifting shadoofs
bobbing toy drinking birds
and turning sakiehs
bringing water to land.

Luxor will speak
for the mute, moving road
echoing in voices
that resound through the tombs
tortured with history
but insisting–"Flow on!"

Onward to Cairo
with a magnetic pull
luring the people
from the villages' bounds
north to the city
where they move in a mass,

City of millions
where the River is
glitter of blue stone
in an evil-eye charm
skyscraper holding
today's wash on her arm
smokestacks of brickworks
framing pyramids' heights,
barbers who shave men
with Nile water and soap
box-camera photogs
with a shop on the bank
rambling casinos
housed in rickety yachts
houseboats and row boats
filled with holiday crowds
packed water taxis
facing barges and dhouws
feluccas tacking from west to the east,
vendors of lettuce
washing leaves till they gleam,
men without houses
bathing cool in the stream.

Life is the River,
and the River is life
spreading like milk ducts
in a mother's full breast,
feeding the Delta
and then flowing to sea,
not to its deathbed
but alive, it remains
coming in fog
and the light autumn rain
ceaselessly flowing
from its birthplace again.

EPILOGUE

OUR FAMILY EXPERIENCED both joyful and challenging moments during our time in Egypt—moments that can best be described as tasting the "water of the Nile." These experiences have woven themselves into the fabric of our identities, suggesting that we are destined to revisit them in our thoughts and actions.

Even after leaving Cairo, the experiences shared with Sonja, Missy, and Troy linger in our minds, shaping our journeys. The lessons learned in resilience and adaptability have resurfaced throughout our lives, teaching us to appreciate diverse cultures and perspectives. While we physically left Cairo, its essence remains ingrained within us, a reminder of a time when we embraced new challenges and found joy in unexpected places.

Floyd died on November 19, 2024. During the last three years of his life, he would frequently ask, "Did you tell the university about me?"

I was not sure which university he was thinking of, but I understood his underlying concern. He wanted to be certain that his achievements would not be forgotten. I have partially fulfilled his request with this book. I only wish we had written it together when he still had clarity about his life-changing Cairo memories.

Floyd had many accomplishments. In his four years at AUC, he played a pivotal role in establishing a new graduate program specifically designed for Egyptian students working within the mass media sector. The initiative not only contributed to the professional development of Egyptian media practitioners but also strengthened AUC's reputation as a leading institution for higher education in the Middle East. Floyd's students applauded his teaching style. He never stayed behind a lectern and looked at notes. He was continually moving on the dais in front of students, making eye contact, giving relevant examples, and encouraging questions and comments. His office door was always open to students. Small groups would come in after class to converse about news topics of the day and communication strategies.

Thanks to his Cairo friend, Bob Ferrar, Floyd was hired in July 1975 by Cleveland State University to teach graduate courses and conduct public opinion research for the US Department of State. Our dream of returning to Colorado came a year later with an invitation to Floyd from the Denver Research Institute to join a research study on the diffusion and impact of citizen band radio on the American public. At the same time, he was also invited to join the faculty at the University of Denver's Department of Speech Communication as an adjunct professor. His Cairo experience provided examples to illustrate the theories he taught.

During our second year back in Colorado, Floyd was diagnosed with Addison's Disease, a rare disorder in which the adrenal glands do not produce enough of the hormone cortisol. This diagnosis solved the mystery of Floyd's lack of fight or flight reactions to the stress of life in Cairo. The low blood pressure, fatigue, stomach upsets, and some lack of awareness to his surroundings were symptoms of this life-threatening disease. Diagnosis of Addison's started Floyd on a lifetime of medication with steroids, which allowed him to live a full professional and personal life.

The next opportunity to use his expertise came when Floyd joined the Solar Energy Research Institute, sponsored by the US Department of Energy. He conducted national studies on the diffusion of solar energy, where he spent four years studying the adoption of passive and active solar systems. In 1981, he coupled his communication background with his widely acknowledged teaching skills to become a regional training manager for the Federal Emergency Management Agency (FEMA). He continued with FEMA's adult training program in disaster prevention until his retirement in 2001.

In Floyd's retirement, he volunteered at the Denver Museum of Nature and Science as a docent on museum exhibits, which included the Titanic and Pharaonic Egypt. His biggest joy in later retirement was facilitating more than twenty courses for Denver University's Osher Lifelong Learning Institute (OLLI). The comment from OLLI South coordinator, Jenny Fortenberry, sums up Floyd's secret to success: "Your enthusiasm, energy, and expertise are felt not just in the classroom but also throughout the entire organization."

▲ ▲ ▲

Sonja, Missy, and Troy utilized their Cairo experience in different ways. Sonja was never quite satisfied with what she thought was a boring life at Heritage High in Littleton, Colorado. Cairo had encouraged this quiet, contemplative oldest daughter to become an adventurer. She decided to go to Caracas, Venezuela, to study Spanish for her junior year while living with a Venezuelan family. She faced many challenges, including some dangerous family situations, but soldiered through them and finished the year despite encouragement from us to come home to Colorado. She majored in Spanish and international studies at the University of Denver and continued for a master's degree in education focusing on English as a second language at the University of Colorado Denver.

While doing a teaching internship at Spring International, she met Pambos Tilliros, a Greek Cypriot student, fell in love, married, and moved to the island of Cyprus. Floyd, Sonja, Missy, Troy, and I traveled to Cyprus for their wedding and visited Cairo and Ma'adi as part of their honeymoon contingent. Sonja taught English at Cyprus College and the European University in Cyprus for more than twenty-five years. They had three sons: Socratis (Cody), Antony, and Loucas. Sonja passed away in 2021 due to non-Hodgkin's lymphoma.

Missy continued to make many friends on her return to the States, in addition to maintaining ties with several of her Cairo buddies. Compassion, optimism, and generosity are attributes that developed during those four important years. She also proved that, like her father, she could soldier through physical pain and illness, situations she would face later in life. After completing Littleton High School, Missy continued her education at Metropolitan State University, graduating with a BS in criminal justice, possibly the result of her "spying" experience on the Egyptian kitchen helpers at the Ma'adi Club.

Her Cairo friend, Elinore Fresh, was the maid of honor at her wedding to Mark Hull, who was born in England, lived in Malta, and immigrated to the United States with his family. They are parents of a son, Benjamin. Missy established the Community Outreach Program at Spring International Language Center, placing hundreds of students from around the world into homestays with American families. Her Egyptian experience informed her counseling of students who were adapting to life in the United States.

Troy's innocence and trust opened doors for the whole family as we moved through life in Cairo. He was too young to consciously be polite and always said what he thought. He did not have to be politically correct. He sat comfortably with the servants and made friends with children from diverse cultures and ethnicities.

Troy maintained his interest in friends from different backgrounds throughout his school days and in his work life. He researched and discovered his own diverse roots in Alaska as the descendant of an Alaskan Inuit chief. Troy graduated from Littleton High School, completed courses in travel and tourism, and was employed as a travel specialist at Globus/Cosmos Tours. He met his wife, Diana, at Globus and married her, and they traveled together in their jobs before settling down to have two children, Kayla and Jesslyn. He and his family travel extensively throughout the world.

My Cairo experience sent me on a whirlwind career. Upon relocating to Denver, I received a one-year fellowship at the Rocky Mountain Women's Institute on the Colorado Women's College campus to develop a book titled *Seven Egyptian Women*. While working on my book, I met two Peace Corps returnees, Robert and Barbara Sample, who started an intensive English as a second language program under the auspices of a Peace Corps training organization. I joined them as an instructor, where I met Pambos Polycarpou, a fellow teacher and a Greek Cypriot.

A few years after our return to Colorado, Bob, Barbara, Pambos, and I had the dream of establishing our own unique ESL program. None of us had the available money to invest in the start-up of a non-profit, and no sponsor. The mortgages on recently acquired houses were our only assets. Floyd was supportive of my involvement and suggested the possibility of second-mortgaging our house. We knew the success of a new venture was uncertain, but after four years of uncertainty in Cairo, we bravely took the risk. The Spring Institute for International Studies became a reality.

Spring Institute later changed its focus to training programs for immigrants and refugees. At that point, Pambos and I were invited by Arapahoe Community College to initiate an ESL program on its campus. We founded Spring International Language Center as a for-profit academic program focusing on preparing international students for college and university. Many of our students were placed by embassies, international organizations, and businesses. Spring International established additional programs at the University of Arkansas in Fayetteville and the Auraria Higher Education campus in metro Denver. Over the years, our ESL schools reflected the world as conflicts developed and economies rose and fell.

Our Egyptian adventure opened our lives to the rest of the world, and our hearts even further to the many students and educators who populated our lives.

Spring International closed its doors in 2024 after forty-four years of recognition as an outstanding program of language education for students around the world. Throughout my directing and teaching career, I continued to write both ESL textbooks and non-fiction books focusing on women of diverse cultures, ages, and backgrounds.

Acknowledgements

My heartfelt gratitude to those who read early drafts and offered encouragement and insight: Marty Dawley, Susan Polycarpou, and Karen Caddoo.

My daughter, Melissa (Missy) Hull, who offered strong support for the endeavor. She also contributed valuable insights from her childhood experiences in Cairo and provided accuracy to some of my faulty recollections.

My son, Troy, who bravely cut through the fog of culture shock to show us what really mattered in our daily lives.

My deep appreciation to book designer, Nick Zelinger of NZ Graphics, for his creativity, insight, and professionalism, and to proof-reader/editor, Jen Z. Marshall, for her thoroughness, dedication, and support.

About the Author

Connie Shoemaker is an award-winning author and educator whose profound experiences in Cairo have significantly shaped her life's work. With a dedicated focus on connecting individuals from diverse cultures and languages, she has spent over forty years in international education. As the co-founder of Spring International Language Center, Connie played a pivotal role in fostering language learning and cultural exchange. Additionally, she serves on the Executive Board of Immigrant Pathways Colorado, further demonstrating her commitment to supporting immigrant communities through education and training.

Notes

Chapter 17: Village Wife, City Woman

1. UNICEF and Demographic and Health Surveys. *Female Genital Mutilation in Egypt: Status and Trends 2021*. Accessed March 22, 2025. https://www.unicef.org/media/128176/file/FGM-Egypt-2021.

2. Egyptian Family Health Survey. *Female Genital Mutilation in Egypt: Status and Trends 2021*. Accessed March 22, 2025. https://www.unicef.org/media/128176/file/FGM-Egypt-2021.

Chapter 19: Weaving Together the Threads

1. "Olga Johanna Miniclier Obituary," Starks Funeral Parlor, May 7, 2020. https://starksfuneral.com/obituary/olga-johanna-miniclier/.

2. Heba Kanso. "Cairo Named Riskiest City for Arab Women Since Arab Spring." Reuters, October 15, 2017. http://www.reuters.com/article/markets/commodities/cairo-named-riskiest-megacity-for-women-worse-since-arab-spring-idUSL8N1LM1H1/.

3. Brian Stelter. "CBS Reporter Recounts a 'Merciless' Assault." *New York Times,* April 28, 2011. https://www.nytimes.com/2011/04/29/business/media/29logan.html.

Glossary of Arabic Words and Phrases

There is no standard method of transliterating Arabic, i.e. representing or spelling an Arabic word in the English alphabet. Words listed here are Cairene pronunciation rather than classical Arabic.

I have tried to explain Arabic words in the context of the sentence following the words, so a parenthetic translation would not interrupt the flow of the story. This glossary will aid the translation when necessary and serve as a review for language learners.

In Modern Standard Arabic, there is no explicit verb for "to be" in the present tense. Instead, sentences are constructed without a linking verb like "am." "is" or "are." For example: *Ana mudarissa* = I am a teacher. There is no word for "am." The reader will notice the missing linking verbs in the speech of characters in the book.

Abadan (Never)

Ahlan bik (You're welcome.)

Ahlan w'sahlan (Welcome)

Ala tool (Hurry up)

Al hamdu lillah (Praise be to God)

Allahu akbar (God is the greatest)

Amrikani (American)

Amrikaniyya (American female)

Ana mish kwayess (I am not well)

Ana mudarissa kaman (I'm a teacher too)

Aroos (bride)

Assalamu alaikum (peace be upon you)

Baksheesh (small tips)

Balady (country man, man of the soil)

Boab (doorkeeper)

Bukra Insha'Allah (God willing, I'll be back tomorrow)

Calèche (horse-drawn carriage)

Darwish (whirling dervish)

Dhouws (Arab lateen-rigged boats)

Djinn (ghosts and demon-like creatures)

Eh, da? (What's that/this? An expression of curiosity)

Emshi (Get away from me)

En sha'allah (God willing)

Etfel izaz (Close up the window)

Etnasher deek rumi (twelve turkeys)

Faransawiyya (French female)

Fellahin (Egyptian peasants)

Feloos kiteer (a lot of money)

Feluccas (boats used by the Egyptians since the beginning of their civilization)

Ful (broad or fava beans)

Galabiya (loose-fitting, ankle--length Egyptian garment)

Gamusa (water buffalo)

Ghee (clarified gamusa butter)

Guineih (Egyptian pound)

Haboob (strong dust storms)

Hadith (the sayings, actions, and approvals of the Prophet Muhammad)

Helwa (beautiful)

Hijab (the traditional head covering)

Iftar (the meal that Muslims eat to break their fast at sunset during Ramadan)

Infitah (the concept of being open to new ideas)

Is salaamu aalekum (peace be unto you)

Istanna shwaya (Wait a minute)

Kalb bebe (puppy)

Kbira (big)

Kefaya (That's enough)

Khamseen (a hot, dry, and dusty wind)

Kulli sana w'inta tayyib (may every year find you well)

Kunafa (a sweet dessert)

Kushari (Egypt's national comfort dish and a widely popular street food)

Kusumik (A curse meaning "go to hell," "F- You")

Kwayiss auwy (excellent)

La-a (No)

La-a Kiff Insarif (No. Stop, Go away)

Ma'adi hena (Ma'adi is here)

Ma'asalama (goodbye)

Ma'alesh (never mind, don't worry, it's ok, etc.)

Ma'sha'allah (Thanks be to God)

Mudarissa (female teacher)

Maghrib (the sunset prayer time)

Makwagi (a laundress)

Mashrabiya (carved wood lattice work)

Melaya (a large black wrap or cloak traditionally worn by Egyptian women)

Min fadlik (please)

Mish magoul (impossible)

Muezzin (man who calls Muslims to prayer)

Naseem (cool breeze)

Piastres (copper-looking coins)

Om (mother)

Oud (a traditional middle eastern stringed instrument)

Rabbina ya khalik (May God protect you)

Ro-ba-bekia (secondhand goods, junk, or used household items)

Sabah el Kheir (good morning)

Saeeda (Greetings of the day)

Sakieh (a waterwheel with a bucket)

Sala'am (peace)

Shadoof (ancient irrigation tool)

Shahmat (egyptian chess)

Shami (Syrian pita bread)

Shukran auwy (thank you so much)

Shwayya baksheesh, min fadlik? (A little tip, please?)

Souks (markets)

Suffragi (general servant)

Sufi (The mystical branch of Islam)

Sunna (the recommended practice)

Suq (a huge bazaar)

Ta'amiya (fava beans with tomato, onions and tahini)

Tahari (clitoral excision)

Talata geneih (Three pounds)

Tarboush (a traditional Turkish hat)

Tayyib (OK)

Xalas (finished)

Ya (hey)

Yasmin (jasmine)

Yemken itneen geneh? (Maybe two pounds?)

Zahgareet (the high-pitched, trilling ululation sound made by women to express joy, celebration, or excitement)

Zibala (garbage, trash, or rubbish)